— EPICURE'S —
APPETISERS
MOCKTAILS & COCKTAILS

POPULAR PRAKASHAN PVT. LTD.
301, Mahalaxmi Chambers
22, Bhulabhai Desai Road
Mumbai 400 026

First Published: 2008

(4229)
ISBN 978-81-7991-481-6

Cover Photograph : Dia Mehta
Food Photography: Arvind Sawant

PRINTED IN INDIA
by Saurabh Printers Pvt. Ltd.
A/16, Sector IV, Noida - 201301

Published by Ramdas Bhatkal
for Popular Prakashan Pvt. Ltd.
301, Mahalaxmi Chambers
22, Bhulabhai Desai Road
Mumbai 400 026

— EPICURE'S —

APPETISERS
MOCKTAILS & COCKTAILS

ASHA KHATAU

Popular Prakashan

www.popularprakashan.com

— Dedication —

To all the students who enjoy my cooking classes and are passionate about cooking.

— Author's Note —

It is said that the first impression is the last impression so, if you want to impress your guests, make that extra effort to try out some of the irresistible, mouth-watering and scrumptious recipes in this book. Here, I have selected the best appetisers and hors d'ouvres from various cuisines of the world. In the book, you will also find your favourite cocktails and mocktails with various fruits and flavours, shots and spirits that are sure to be the life of a party.

There are recipes of starters, some of which are light and quick to make and others that are elaborate and substantial. It is a good idea to combine appetisers of different cuisines for the same occasion, making sure that they complement each other. It is also important to keep in mind what time of the day or what occasion you are planning for, so that you can choose from a variety of mocktails and cocktails that will suit the occasion.

Drinks should complement the food you are serving. For example, along with Mexican starters like quesadillas or corn salsa, you could serve a Margarita or a Sangrita. If you are selecting starters for a formal cocktail party, make sure that you choose those that are not messy. If you are planning a cocktails and starters party, you must choose substantial starters with an elaborate punch bowl that can see people through the evening. The Appetiser Bar will go very well with the Planter's Punch Bowl or Sparkling Grape Juice Punch.

Some of the recipes, like the Appetiser Torte and Sun-dried Tomato Pesto Torta, are designed with the idea that they can be prepared a day ahead if one is pressed for time.

So bienvenidos to a new chapter in entertaining with style!

ENJOY!!!!!

— Acknowledgements —

I sincerely thank the One above for giving me the ability and capacity to write yet another book in my Epicure Series. I want to thank my mother-in law, Leela Khatau, for giving me constant encouragement and support in everything I do. I remember with gratitude, my late mother, Sudha Sampat, for the encouragement and courage that she gave me all my life. I sincerely thank my husband, Mahendra Khatau, for his constructive suggestions and moral support in whatever I do. Help from my three children, Priya, Shreya and Manish is always at hand - I thank them from the bottom of my heart. My special thanks to my sister-in-law, Ameeta Thackersey, for always standing by my side and helping in every way needed. I would also like to thank Janki Khatau, Niti Desai, Kanchan Vaswani, Jayshreebhabhi, Dhruti, and Devhutiben for helping me during the photo shoot. I appreciate and thank my dedicated staff Gopinath, Mahadev, Santosh, Naresh, G. Kateria, Dattu, Ankush and Jha who are always willing to work and help. I thank everyone at Popular Prakashan associated with this book, for their help and co-operation.

Finally, I sincerely thank Dia Mehta for taking out precious time to shoot the photograph for the cover of the book.

— Contents —

APPETISERS

MOCKTAILS

COCKTAILS

Appetisers

Call them by whatever name you wish - antipasti, dimsum, starters or hors d'oeuvres- these delicious bites of food are perfect for whetting the appetite for the main course in a party menu! They set the stage for a party and create a mood of bonhomie.

Almond-Mushroom Pâté

INGREDIENTS **Serves 6**

2 tbsp	butter
¼ cup	finely chopped onion,
1 large clove	garlic, finely chopped
1½ cups	fresh mushrooms, sliced
1 tsp	fresh tarragon, finely chopped
1 cup	blanched almonds
1 tbsp	lemon juice
1 tbsp	Worcestershire sauce
½ tbsp	white pepper powder
2 tbsp	cream cheese

Salt to taste
Fresh parsley sprigs to line the tin

To garnish
Slivered almonds

To serve
Crusty French bread or crackers

METHOD

In a large frying pan, melt butter; add onion, garlic and mushrooms. Sauté till tender but not brown. Add tarragon and cook till soft. Remove from heat, cool slightly and transfer to a food processor or blender along with the rest of the ingredients except the cream cheese. Blend till smooth. Turn out into a bowl and fold in the cream cheese. Pour the mixture into a serving bowl and chill; or pour into a mould lined with chopped parsley and freeze till set. Unmould onto a serving platter, garnish with slivered almonds and serve with bread or crackers.

Asparagus Tarts

INGREDIENTS **Makes 12 tarts**

2–3 tbsp	Mayonnaise (page 230)
1 tbsp	mustard paste
1 tbsp	chopped fresh parsley
1 large clove	garlic, chopped fine
1 cup	grated processed cheese
250 gms	fresh asparagus spears, cooked and chilled
¼ cup	finely chopped red pepper
12 small	tart cases

Salt and pepper to taste

METHOD

In a small bowl, mix together mayonnaise, mustard paste, parsley, garlic, grated cheese, salt and pepper. Beat until smooth. Chop asparagus spears into half-inch pieces and add along with the red pepper to the cheese mixture. Spoon 1-2 tablespoons of the mixture into each tart case and bake at 200°C/400°F/Gas Mark 6 for 5-7 minutes or till the cheese melts. Serve at once.

Appetiser Puffs

INGREDIENTS **Makes 16-20 puffs**

1½ cups	plain flour
1 tsp	salt
1 cup	butter
½ cup	sour cream
2 tbsp	grated Parmesan cheese
2 tbsp	chopped spring onions
2 tbsp	chopped fresh mushrooms
2 tbsp	chopped olives
½ tsp	pepper
½ tsp	chilli flakes
½ tsp	mustard paste
1 tbsp	chopped fresh basil leaves
Salt to taste	

METHOD

Mix flour and salt; cut butter into the flour with 2 knives, or mix lightly with your fingertips, until the mixture resembles breadcrumbs. Blend in sour cream and gather the dough to form a ball. Divide the dough into four parts. Wrap in cling film and chill in a refrigerator. Preheat the oven to 180°C/350°F/Gas Mark 4. On a floured surface, roll each part of the dough into a 12-inch x 6-inch rectangle. Mix grated Parmesan cheese, spring onions, mushrooms and olives in a small bowl. Add salt, pepper, chilli flakes, mustard paste and basil. Toss gently to mix. Sprinkle one-fourth of the mixture all over the rolled dough. Fold it over twice to form a smaller rectangle, pressing the edges down. Repeat till all the four parts are folded. Place on an ungreased rectangular baking sheet in the oven for 20-25 minutes. Remove from the oven, cut each rectangle into 4-5 slices and serve.

Appetiser Torte

INGREDIENTS **Serves 12**

400 gms	cream cheese
½ cup	crumbled cottage cheese
8 slices	Cheddar cheese
¾ cup	Pesto Sauce (page 233)
½ cup	sun-dried tomatoes, soaked and chopped
¼ cup	toasted pine nuts

To garnish

Sliced red pepper, sprigs of parsley and a few toasted pine nuts

To serve

Sliced and toasted crusty bread

METHOD

Wet a piece of muslin and line a 6-inch round or 6-inch triangular mould with it, allowing the cloth to extend over the sides. Beat cream cheese and cottage cheese until very creamy and smooth. In the prepared pan, layer ingredients as follows: 1 cup cream cheese mixture, 3-4 cheese slices, one-third cup pesto, 3-4 cheese slices; 1 cup cream cheese mixture, sun-dried tomatoes, toasted pine nuts, one-third cup pesto and the remaining cheese mixture.

Fold the cloth over to cover the mould completely and refrigerate overnight. Unwrap the mould and turn out onto a serving platter. Garnish with red pepper slices, parsley and pine nuts. Serve with toasted bread.

Note: Provide a small paté knife for easy serving.

Appetiser Bar

At the bar, make all the dips and spreads and arrange them at the table decoratively. Serve with plenty of toasted breads, lavash, bread sticks, salted crackers, chips, taco chips, vegetable crudités etc.

FOR THE DIPS

Sun-dried Tomato and Basil Spread: **Makes 1 cup**
Soak 1/4 cup sun-dried tomatoes in hot water for 20 minutes. Blend with 1/4 cup olive oil and 100 grams cream cheese, until creamy. Fold in 1/4 cup of chopped basil.

Spinach Dip: **Makes 2 1/2 cups**
Combine 2 cups chopped and blanched spinach with 2 cups Sour Cream (page 234), 1 cup Mayonnaise (page 230), 1 packet vegetable soup mix, 1 cup chopped water chestnuts, 2 chopped spring onions stems and salt to taste.

Baked Mozzarella-Jalapeño Dip: **Serves 6**
Mix together 1 1/4 cups grated mozzarella cheese, 1/2 cup grated Parmesan cheese, 2-3 cloves crushed garlic, 1/4 cup chopped black olives, 2 tablespoons each finely chopped onion and jalapeño chillies, 1/2 tsp garlic salt and a dash of Tabasco sauce. Spread the mixture in a greased baking dish and bake for 15 minutes.

Cheese and Olive Welsh Rarebit: **Serves 12**
Mix together 1/2 cup grated processed cheese, 1/4 cup finely chopped olives, 2 soaked and chopped sun-dried tomatoes, 2 tablespoons Mayonnaise (page 230), 1/2 tsp mustard powder, salt and pepper. Spread the mixture over toasted bread pieces, garnish with sliced olives and bake in a preheated oven at 200°C/400°F/Gas Mark 6 for 5-6 minutes or until cheese melts. Serve hot.

Roasted Red Pepper and Walnut Spread: **Makes 1 1/4 cups**
Blend together 1 large roasted red pepper, 200 grams cream cheese, 1/4 cup toasted walnuts, 2-3 cloves crushed garlic and 2 tablespoons olive oil until smooth. Transfer to a bowl and sprinkle paprika.

Appetiser Bar

Baked Corn Salsa

INGREDIENTS **Serves 4-6**

1 tbsp	oil
2-3 cloves	garlic, crushed
2 medium	onions, finely chopped
½ cup	finely chopped red or green peppers
2 medium	tomatoes, finely chopped
1 cup	boiled corn kernels
2-3 tbsp	finely chopped jalapeño chillies
2-3 tbsp	finely chopped coriander leaves
1 tsp	cumin powder
1 tsp	chilli powder
1 tsp	taco seasoning
1 tsp	oregano
¼ cup	grated Cheddar cheese
2	7-inch tortillas, brushed with butter and cut into strips

Salt to taste

To serve
Taco chips and Red Salsa (page 234)

METHOD

Preheat the oven to 180°C/350°F/Gas Mark 4. Heat oil in a small frying pan and fry garlic, onions and peppers for two minutes. Remove from heat and transfer to a bowl. Add tomatoes, corn, jalapeños, coriander leaves and all the spices and salt. Toss to mix and transfer to a shallow baking dish. Cover the top with grated cheese. Arrange prepared tortilla strips on top. Bake for 8-10 minutes. Serve hot with taco chips and salsa.

Asparagus and Parmesan on Potato Roesti

Baked Vegetable Cups

Baked Corn Salsa

Asparagus with Herbed Cheese on Toast

INGREDIENTS **Serves 8**

500 gms	fresh asparagus spears, trimmed and chopped
3-4 medium	onions, sliced and halved
1 cup	crumbled ricotta or cottage cheese
2 tbsp	finely chopped mixed herbs of your choice
6-8 slices	French bread (baguette), toasted
1 tbsp	oilve oil
¼ tsp	salt
¼ tsp	pepper

METHOD

Drop asparagus spears and onion slices into a large saucepan of boiling water; cook for 3-4 minutes. Drain and plunge into ice water; drain well again, pat dry with paper towels and set aside. Combine the cheese and herbs in a bowl; stir well. Spread cheese mixture evenly over the slices of bread and set aside. Heat the oil in a non-stick frying pan. Add onion, salt and pepper and sauté for 3-4 minutes until brown. Add asparagus and heat through. Top the bread slices with the mixture and place briefly under a grill till the topping is bubbly. Serve at once.

Asparagus Wraps

INGREDIENTS **Serves 4**

2-3 tbsp	Mayonnaise (page 230)
1 tbsp	grainy mustard
1 tbsp	chopped parsley
8	3-inch round tortillas
8 slices	cheese
8 fresh	asparagus spears, blanched

Salt and pepper to taste
Melted butter

To serve
Ranch dressing

METHOD

Whisk mayonnaise, mustard, parsley, salt and pepper in a small bowl. Spread the mayonnaise mixture on each tortilla. Cut each cheese slice a little smaller than the tortillas and press onto each tortilla. Place one asparagus spear at the end of the tortilla and roll up like a Swiss roll. Seal the edge and secure with a toothpick. Either serve this way, or brush each one with a little butter and toast in an oven till crisp. Serve with ranch dressing.

Avocado Appetiser Cheesecake

INGREDIENTS Serves 6-8

150 gms	cheese crackers, crushed
1 cup	Sour Cream (page 234)
1 tbsp	melted butter
1 tsp	dried mixed herbs
1 cup	mashed avocado
½ cup	cream cheese
1 small	onion
1 small	capsicum, quartered
2 cloves	garlic
2 tbsp	lemon juice
1 tsp	Worcestershire sauce
1 tsp	salt
1 tsp	chopped chillies
1 tsp	mustard
2 tsp	unflavoured gelatine
¼ cup	Vegetable Stock (page 166)

To garnish

¼ cup sliced olives and chopped chives and parsley

To serve

Wholewheat crackers or toasted bread

METHOD

Mix three-fourth of the cracker crumbs, 2 tablespoons sour cream and the melted butter. Line the bottom of a 9-inch loose-bottomed pan with the mixture. Set aside. Dissolve the gelatine in the stock. Process the rest of the ingredients in a blender to a smooth paste. Turn out into the lined tin and chill until set. Top with remaining cracker crumbs. Garnish with olives and herbs. Cut into wedges and serve with crackers or toasted bread.

Avocado Cups

INGREDIENTS **Makes 16 cups**

4 slices	bread
2-3 tbsp	melted butter
1/4 tsp	mustard
1 tsp + 2 tbsp	lemon juice
2 medium	avocados, peeled and mashed
1/2 cup	thick yogurt
1 tbsp	crushed garlic
1 tbsp	chopped chives
1 small	tomato, blanched, deseeded and chopped
Salt to taste	

METHOD

Preheat the oven to 180°C/350°F/Gas Mark 4. Trim the crust of the bread and cut each slice into 4 pieces. Mix the melted butter with mustard, 1 teaspoon lemon juice and a pinch of salt. Spread this mixture on each square. With your index finger, lightly press the squares into miniature muffin cups. Bake for 10-15 minutes. Remove from the oven and set aside to cool. When completely cold, unmould and store in an airtight container.

Sprinkle 2 tablespoons lemon juice over the mashed avocado. Add the remaining ingredients. Mix well and chill in a refrigerator for 1-2 hours. Just before serving, spoon the avocado mixture into the toasted cups and serve.

Baby Potato and Feta Cheese Fondue

INGREDIENTS **Serves 6**

200 gms	feta cheese or goat cheese
1 tbsp	cornflour
1 cup	buttermilk
2-3 tbsp	chopped chives
1 tbsp	finely chopped thyme
1 tbsp	finely chopped tarragon
1 tbsp	finely chopped parsley
20	baby potatoes, boiled in salted water and peeled

Salt and pepper to taste

METHOD

Mix feta cheese, cornflour and buttermilk in a bowl and place the bowl on top of a pan of boiling water, stirring till the cheese melts. Remove and add all the herbs, salt and pepper. Mix well. Use this as a warm dip for the potatoes. Alternatively, you can use bread cubes for dipping.

Asparagus and Parmesan on Potato Roesti

INGREDIENTS **Serve 6**

100 gms	butter
500 gms	potatoes, peeled and grated
8-10	fresh or tinned asparagus spears
¼ cup	grated Parmesan cheese

Salt and pepper to taste

For the parsley sauce

½ cup	Vegetable Stock (page 166)
2 tbsp	finely chopped parsley
2 tbsp	butter
2 tbsp	plain flour
1 cup	milk
3 tbsp	thick cream

Salt and pepper to taste

METHOD

For the parsley sauce

Process the stock with parsley in a blender. Melt butter in a saucepan; add the flour and cook for 1-2 minutes. Add parsley-flavoured stock and stir until smooth. Whisk in the milk and return the pan to heat. Cook until thick, stirring occasionally. Stir in the cream, salt and pepper and heat gently. Remove from heat and keep warm.

For the roesti

Melt 2 tablespoons of butter in a heavy frying pan. Drain the potatoes completely and pat dry. Place 4-5 handfuls of grated potato on the pan. Cover and cook on low heat till the undersides are golden brown; turn over and cook the other side. Repeat until all the potatoes are done this way. Transfer to a greased baking dish and keep warm.

Preheat the oven to 180°C/350°F/Gas Mark 4. Cut asparagus into 1-inch pieces. (Boil if using fresh asparagus and drain if using tinned ones). Toss with Parmesan cheese, salt and pepper. Spoon a few asparagus tips on each roesti, top with parsley sauce and bake for 4-5 minutes. Serve at once.

Baked Millet Cake
(Bajri no Handvo)

INGREDIENTS **Serves 6-8**

2 cups	coarsely ground millet flour
1½ cups	thick, sour buttermilk
1 tsp	soda bicarbonate
1 tbsp	hot oil
1 cup	fresh fenugreek leaves, washed and chopped
½ cup	shelled and boiled green peas
½ cup	semolina
1 large	tomato, chopped
1 tbsp	green chilli-ginger paste
1 tsp	red chilli powder
1 tsp	sesame seeds

A pinch of turmeric powder
Salt to taste

For the tempering

4 tbsp	oil
1 tsp	mustard seeds
2	1-inch cinnamon sticks
2	cloves
2	dried red button chillies

A pinch of asafoetida
A few curry leaves

To garnish
Finely chopped coriander

To serve
Green Chutney (page 236) mixed with yogurt

METHOD

Soak millet flour in sour buttermilk for 4 hours. Preheat the oven to 180°C/350°F/Gas Mark 4. Mix soda bicarbonate with hot oil and add to the millet flour mixture along with the remaining ingredients and mix well. Grease a 6-cup capacity ovenproof dish and pour in the millet mixture.

For the tempering

Heat oil in a small pan; add the mustard seeds. When they begin to crackle, add the remaining ingredients and pour the sizzling spices evenly over the millet mixture.

Bake the handvo till golden brown. Cut into squares, garnish with chopped coriander and serve hot with green chutney.

Basil and Cheese Spread

INGREDIENTS **Serves 4-6**

5-6	fresh basil leaves
2 cloves	garlic
½ tsp	salt
180 gms	cream cheese spread
½ cup	grated Parmesan cheese
½ cup	chopped walnuts
¼ cup	olive oil

To serve

Crackers or toasted sliced French bread (baguette)

METHOD

Finely chop basil and garlic along with the salt in a blender. Add the remaining ingredients and blend until smooth. Transfer to a serving bowl and place in a refrigerator to chill. Serve with crackers or toasted French bread.

Baked Vegetable Cupcakes

INGREDIENTS **Makes 10-12 cupcakes**

4-5 slices	white bread with crusts
1 cup	milk
400 gms	potatoes, boiled and mashed
1 cup	mixed vegetables, boiled
1 cup	boiled corn kernels
½ tsp	garam masala
1 tbsp	lemon juice
1 tbsp	ginger-chilli paste
1 tbsp	chopped fresh coriander
1 tbsp	oil
½ cup	breadcrumbs
¼ cup	tomato ketchup

Salt and sugar to taste

For the tempering

1-2 tbsp	oil
½ tsp	mustard seeds
½ tsp	sesame seeds
½ tsp	asafoetida
2-3	dried red chillies, chopped

A few curry leaves

To serve

Green Chutney (page 236) or tomato ketchup

METHOD

Preheat the oven to 180°C/350°F/Gas Mark 4. Soak the bread slices in milk and mash into a pulp when soft. Mix together the mashed potato, bread pulp, boiled vegetables and corn. Add salt, sugar, garam masala, lemon juice, ginger-chilli paste and coriander and mix well.

Grease small muffin or cupcake moulds with a little oil and line them with breadcrumbs. Fill half the mould with the potato mixture. Spread 1 teaspoon of tomato ketchup on top and spoon in some more of the mixture. Smooth the surface and sprinkle some breadcrumbs.

For the tempering

Heat oil in a small pan. Add the mustard seeds and when the seeds begin to crackle, add sesame seeds, asafoetida, curry leaves and chillies.

Spoon a little of the tempering on top of each cupcake and bake in the oven till golden brown. Remove from the moulds and serve hot with green chutney or tomato ketchup.

Balsamic Mushrooms

INGREDIENTS **Serves 4**

2 cloves	garlic, crushed
3 tbsp	olive oil
250 gms	mushrooms, washed and sliced
1½ tbsp	balsamic vinegar
1½ tbsp	white wine (optional)
1 tbsp	finely chopped parsley

Salt and pepper to taste

To serve

Crusty bread slices

METHOD

Sauté the garlic in olive oil for 1 or 2 minutes. Add mushrooms and cook for 2 more minutes, stirring occasionally. Stir in vinegar and wine. Season with salt and pepper to taste. Add parsley and remove from heat. Serve hot or cold with crusty bread.

Baked South-Western Dip

INGREDIENTS

Serves 6-8

For the crust

2 cups	crushed nacho chips
3 tbsp	melted butter

For the filling

1 cup	cream cheese
½ cup	cottage cheese
½ cup	beaten fresh cream
1 cup	grated Cheddar or Monterey Jack cheese
¼ cup	chopped jalapeño chillies
¼ cup	chopped onions
1 tbsp	Tabasco sauce
1 tbsp	lemon juice
1 clove	garlic, finely chopped
½ cup	spring onions
½ cup	diced tomatoes
½ cup	olives

Salt and pepper to taste

To serve

Crisp tortilla chips

METHOD

For the crust

Mix nacho chips and butter and press the mixture into an 8-inch round pie dish. Bake for 10 minutes at 170°C/325°F/Gas Mark 3. Set aside to cool.

For the filling

Preheat the oven to 180°C/350°F/Gas Mark 4. Beat cream cheese, cottage cheese and fresh cream together until smooth. Add the grated cheese, jalapeño chillies, onion, Tabasco, lemon juice, garlic, salt and pepper. Spread the mixture in the prepared pie dish and bake for 20 minutes. Cool for 5-10 minutes and cover the top with spring onions, tomatoes and olives. Chill for 2-3 hours. Serve with crisp tortilla chips.

Bistro Onion Pizzetta

INGREDIENTS — **Serves 8**

1 tbsp	butter
1 tbsp	olive oil
1 tsp	roasted and crushed garlic
3 large	onions, halved and thinly sliced
1 tsp	salt
1 tsp	pepper
8-10 small	pizza bases, trimmed and brushed with olive oil
2 cups	grated Cheddar cheese
1 tsp	cornflour
½ cup	milk
¼ cup	cream

METHOD

Preheat the oven to 200°C/400°F/Gas Mark 6. Melt butter and olive oil together in a frying pan. Add roasted garlic, onions, salt and pepper. Cook till the onions are golden brown. Set aside to cool. Slightly warm the pizza bases in the oven. Remove and spread the onion mixture evenly on each base. In a bowl, mix the cheese and cornflour. Stir in the milk and cream. Pour 2 tablespoons of the mixture on each pizza base over the onions and bake for 10-12 minutes. Remove and cool slightly before serving.

Broccoli and Almond Dip

INGREDIENTS

Serves 4-6

1 tbsp	olive oil
1 small	onion, chopped
1 clove	garlic, chopped
¼ cup	blanched almonds
2 cups	blanched broccoli florets
¾ cup	cottage cheese
¼ cup	thick yogurt

Salt and pepper to taste

To serve

Melba toast

METHOD

Heat oil over medium heat and fry onion and garlic until soft. Add almonds and three-fourths of the broccoli florets. Cook until tender. Remove from heat and set aside to cool. Blend cottage cheese and yogurt till smooth. Add salt, pepper and the cooled broccoli mixture. Continue to blend until smooth. Turn out into a bowl and fold in the remaining one-fourth cup of broccoli. Serve warm with Melba toast.

Broccoli Cups

INGREDIENTS **Serves 6**

12 tbsp	mustard paste
1 tbsp	honey or sugar
1 tbsp	vinegar
1 tsp	chilli flakes
12 thin	slices of bread, crusts removed
1-2 tbsp	melted butter
2 cups	broccoli florets, chopped into small pieces and blanched
1 cup	grated processed cheese
1/4 cup	cream
1 cup	milk
1/2 cup	sifted flour
1/2 tsp	salt
1/2 tsp	oil
1 tsp	dried mixed herbs
A pinch of salt	

METHOD

Preheat the oven to 180°C/350°F/Gas Mark 4. In a bowl, mix together mustard, honey, vinegar, chilli flakes and salt. Brush the bread slices with a little butter and press them to line cupcake or muffin tins. Bake for 8-10 minutes. Remove the toast cups, arrange on a baking sheet and set aside. Toss broccoli with grated cheese. Beat the cream, stir in milk and add the flour, salt, mixed herbs and oil together. Bring to a boil in a saucepan and gently fold in the broccoli and cheese mixture a little at a time. Cook until thick. Spoon the mixture into each toast cup and bake till golden brown. Serve hot with the honey-mustard sauce.

Buttermilk Batter-fried Onion Rings

INGREDIENTS **Serves 4**

2 large	onions, cut into ½-inch thick slices
1 cup	plain flour
1 tsp	baking powder
½ tsp	salt
1 tbsp	powdered sugar
1½ cups	beaten yogurt
1 tbsp	melted butter

Oil for deep-frying

To serve

Sour Cream (page 234)

METHOD

Separate the onion layers into rings and set aside. Sift the flour with baking powder, salt and powdered sugar. Add the yogurt and mix into a smooth batter. Add melted butter and mix well. Chill in a refrigerator for half an hour. Pour 2 inches of oil into a frying pan and heat till the oil smokes. Lower the heat. Dip onion rings into the batter till well coated. Drop the rings into the hot oil and fry a few at a time until golden. Drain on a paper towel and serve immediately.

Note: If you like crunchy rings, roll in breadcrumbs after dipping them in the batter and deep-fry.

Caesar Salad Tacos

INGREDIENTS **Serves 12**

8 cups	mixed romaine and iceberg lettuce, washed and cut into squares
½ cup	grated Cheddar cheese
1 medium	avocado, peeled, stoned and diced
½ cup	boiled black beans
½ cup	boiled corn kernels
¼ cup	finely chopped jalapeño chillies
1/3 cup	Garlic Mayonnaise (page 230)
¼ cup	Red Salsa (page 234)
12	taco shells, warmed
2 medium	tomatoes, finely chopped
Salt to taste	

METHOD

Combine mixed lettuce, half the cheese, avocado, beans, corn and jalapeño chillies in a large bowl. Combine mayonnaise, salsa and salt in a small bowl; mix well. Pour the mayonnaise mixture over the lettuce mixture and toss well. Fill each taco shell with the salad mixture; top with remaining cheese and chopped tomatoes. Serve immediately.

Cheese and Olive Cigars

INGREDIENTS

Makes 16-20 servings

1 cup	grated Cheddar cheese
1/4 cup	finely chopped olives
1	finely chopped spring onion stem
1/2 tsp	dried oregano
1 clove	garlic, chopped fine
6 sheets	phyllo pastry or puff pastry
1/4 cup	melted butter

METHOD

In a small bowl, combine cheese, olives, spring onion, oregano and garlic; set aside. Lightly grease a baking sheet and preheat the oven to 190°C/375°F/Gas Mark 5. Place 1 sheet of phyllo pastry on a flat surface. Cover remaining sheets with a damp cloth to prevent them from drying out. Brush the pastry with melted butter. Top with 2 more phyllo sheets, brushing each one with butter. Spoon half the cheese mixture in the centre and carefully roll up into a tight roll. Place seam side down on the prepared baking sheet. Brush the top with butter. Repeat with remaining phyllo sheets and filling. Bake for 10-15 minutes until golden brown. Serve warm.

Cajun Potato Wedges

INGREDIENTS **Serves 4-6**

¼ cup	salad oil
4 medium	potatoes
2 tbsp	Cajun Spice Mix (recipe follows)

To serve
Red Salsa (page 234) or Sour Cream (page 234)

METHOD

Preheat the oven to 190°C/375°F/Gas Mark 5. Pour half an inch of oil into a baking dish and place in the oven for about 5 minutes until hot. Cut the potatoes with the skin into wedges. Arrange in the baking dish in the hot oil and bake for 10 minutes. Remove and sprinkle Cajun spice mix over the potatoes until well-coated. Bake again for 20-25 minutes, turning occasionally, until golden brown. Drain and serve immediately with salsa or sour cream.

Cajun Spice Mix **Makes 4 tbsp**

Mix together 1 tbsp garlic powder, 1 tbsp onion powder, 2 tsp black or white pepper, 2 tsp dried thyme, ½ tsp dried oregano and 1½ tsp chilli flakes. Fill in an airtight bottle and use as required.

Cajun-style Potato Nuggets

INGREDIENTS **Serves 6-8**

1 packet	dry soup mix (onion, tomato, vegetable or asparagus)
½ cup	toasted breadcrumbs
1 tsp	Cajun Spice Mix (page 39)
½ tsp	black pepper
1 cup	mashed potato
1 cup	crumbled cottage cheese
1 cup	boiled corn kernels

Salt to taste
Oil for frying

To serve

Tomato ketchup and mustard paste

METHOD

In a large bowl, combine dry soup mix, breadcrumbs, Cajun spice mix, salt and pepper. In another bowl, mix together potato, cottage cheese and corn. Make walnut-sized balls of the mixture and roll in the dry mixture. Either deep-fry in hot oil or pierce with a candy stick, shape like a lollipop and roast on a hot griddle in a little oil. Serve with tomato ketchup and mustard paste.

Caramelised Onion Dip

INGREDIENTS **Serves 6**

3 medium	onions, sliced
1 tbsp	butter
1 tbsp	sesame oil
½ cup	Mayonnaise (page 230)
½ cup	Sour Cream (page 234)
1 tsp	red pepper flakes
¼ tsp	salt
¼ tsp	pepper
A few drops of	Tabasco sauce

To serve
Crackers or chips

METHOD

Sauté onions in butter and sesame oil until caramelised (golden brown), for about 20 minutes. Cool and combine with the remaining ingredients. Mix well and chill for 1 hour. Serve with crackers or chips.

Caramelised Onion Parcels

INGREDIENTS

Makes 10

2 tbsp	olive oil + for greasing
3 large	onions, halved and sliced
2-3	jalapeño chillies, finely chopped
1 tsp	black pepper
¼ cup	sliced olives
2 cups	processed cheese
¼ kg	puff pastry or phyllo dough
¼ cup	clarified butter
Salt to taste	

METHOD

In a large frying pan, heat olive oil and sauté the onions and the chillies until the onions caramelise. Let the mixture cool; stir in salt, pepper, olives and cheese and mix well. Roll out the pastry dough, cut into 3-inch x 5-inch sections and brush the tops with clarified butter. Spoon a little onion mixture in the centre of each rectangle and fold like an envelope. Seal the edges and place on a greased baking tray. Brush the top lightly with clarified butter. Bake in a hot oven at 190°C/375°F/Gas Mark 5 for 20 minutes or till golden brown. Serve hot.

Carrot and Cheese Pinwheels

INGREDIENTS Serves 6-8

1 cup	softened cream cheese
2 small	carrots, grated
½ cup	toasted ground walnuts
¼ cup	Mayonnaise (page 230)
¼ cup	chopped green capsicum
¼ cup	chopped cucumber
1 tbsp	finely chopped spring onion
1 tbsp	finely chopped parsley
6-8	bread slices, crusts removed

Salt, pepper and mustard to taste

METHOD

Mix together all the ingredients except the bread in a small bowl. Chill for 1 hour. Spread the mixture on the bread slices and either cut into triangles or roll up into cylinders. Secure the ends with toothpicks. Cover and refrigerate until ready to serve.

Caesar Sandwiches

INGREDIENTS

Serves 6

12 slices — Italian bread
¼ cup — butter, softened
2 tbsp — freshly chopped parsley
¼ cup — grated Parmesan cheese

For the Caesar dressing

¼ cup — Mayonnaise (page 230)
1 clove — garlic, minced
2 tsp — Dijon mustard
1 tsp — lemon juice
1 tsp — Worcestershire sauce
Salt and pepper to taste

METHOD

Preheat the oven to 190°C/375°F/Gas Mark 5. Combine all the ingredients for the Caesar dressing in a bowl. Add butter and beat until creamy. Add parsley and cheese and mix well. Spread the mixture on each slice of bread and sandwich two slices together. Wrap the sandwiches in foil and bake for 20 minutes. Open the foil wrapping and bake again for 10 more minutes until the edges are crisp. Serve hot.

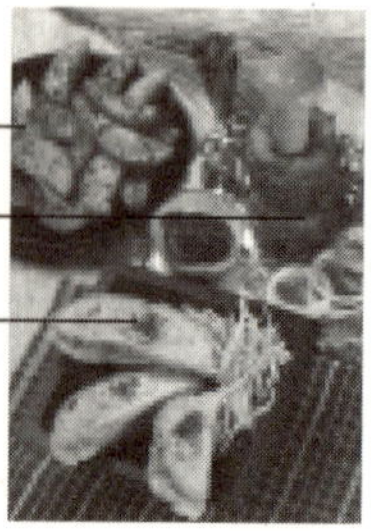

Cajun Potato Wedges
Buttermilk Batter-Fried Onion Rings
Caesar Sandwiches

Chickpea Falafels with Harissa

INGREDIENTS

Makes 12 falafels

150 gms	chickpeas, soaked overnight and cooked
1 medium	onion, chopped
3 cloves	garlic, peeled
¼ cup	chopped parsley
½ tsp	soda bicarbonate
2 tsp	coriander-cumin powder
1 tbsp	plain flour + to coat the patties

Salt and pepper to taste
Oil for deep-frying

For the harissa

100 gms	dried red chillies, roasted
6 cloves	garlic
1 tsp	caraway seeds
1 tsp	salt
1 tsp	coriander powder
1 tsp	pepper
1 tsp	cumin powder

METHOD

Drain the chickpeas, reserving 1 tablespoon of cooking liquid. Place chickpeas in a blender; add onion, garlic, parsley, reserved liquid, soda bicarbonate, spices, salt and pepper. Blend until smooth. Place in a glass bowl and refrigerate until firm. Shape into 12 patties. Dust lightly with flour and deep-fry in hot oil, turning frequently, until browned and crisp. Drain on paper towels. Serve with harissa.

For the harissa

Makes 1 cup

Grind chillies and garlic coarsely. Add the remaining ingredients. Fill the mixture in a jar and store in refrigerator.

To use this mixture as a condiment or spice mix, simply mix equal quantity of harissa with olive oil and blend to a paste.

Chilli-Cheese Popcorn

Cheese Wontons

Chickpea Falafels with Harissa

Carrot and Cheese Pinwheels

Cheese Papad Rolls

INGREDIENTS **Serves 6**

4 thin large	moong dal papads
250 gms	processed cheese, cut into 1-inch sticks
1 tsp	chilli powder
Oil for deep-frying	

METHOD

Place the papads on a flat surface and moisten with just enough water to soften them. Cut each one into 1-inch strips. Place a cheese stick at the edge of each papad strip and lightly roll it up. Secure the ends with a toothpick. Holding one end of the toothpick, deep-fry the roll in hot oil. Remove and drain on a paper towel. Sprinkle with chilli powder and serve hot.

Cheese Tartlets with Onion Marmalade

INGREDIENTS

Serves 6

12-14	tartlet cases
½ cup	grated Gouda or Gruyère cheese
2 tbsp	double cream

Salt, pepper and mustard to taste

For the onion marmalade

3 tbsp	olive oil
450 gms	onions, thinly sliced
3 tbsp	brown sugar
2 tbsp	wine vinegar

To garnish

Finely chopped parsley

METHOD

For the marmalade

Heat olive oil in a heavy skillet and add the onions and sugar. Cook over medium heat, stirring occasionally, till the onions caramelise. Add the vinegar and cook till the mixture turns gooey. Remove from heat and allow to cool completely.

For the tartlets

Preheat the oven to 150°C/300°F/Gas Mark 2. Arrange the tartlets on a baking sheet. Toss cheese with salt, pepper and mustard and mix in the double cream. Spoon 2 teaspoons of the cheese mixture into each tartlet, top with a teaspoon of the onion marmalade and bake for 4-5 minutes till the cheese melts. Remove the tartlets from the oven and allow to cool slightly. Garnish with parsley and serve warm.

Cheese Wontons

INGREDIENTS **Serves 6**

2-3 cloves	garlic, crushed
1 tbsp	olive oil
1 tbsp	basil paste
½ tsp	salt
½ tsp	pepper
½ tsp	dried oregano
2 tbsp	chopped pine nuts
100 gms	mozzarella cheese, cubed
10-12	wonton wrappers

A little flour paste to stick the wrappers
Oil for deep-frying

To serve
Tomato-chilli sauce

METHOD

In a small bowl, combine garlic, olive oil, basil paste, salt, pepper, oregano and pine nuts. Mix together with a fork. Add the cheese cubes and toss gently to coat. Set aside for 10-15 minutes. Take one wrapper, place 1 marinated cheese cube in the centre and fold the opposite ends to make a triangle; seal the edges with flour paste. Lift the two ends and fold them over to meet in the shape of a cap. Seal the tips with the paste. Alternatively, you could shape them like bags or potlis. Arrange them on a tray to dry out and then deep-fry them in hot oil until crisp. Serve immediately with tomato-chilli sauce.

Cheese-Chilli Puffs

INGREDIENTS **Makes 60 puffs**

1¾ cups	plain flour, sifted
1 tsp	salt
½ tsp	crushed garlic
1 tsp	mixed dried herbs
½ cup	butter
½ cup	Sour Cream (page 234)
1 cup	grated Cheddar cheese
¼ cup	finely chopped jalapeño chillies

METHOD

In a medium bowl, combine the flour, salt, garlic and herbs. Add the butter and mix with a fork until the mixture is crumbly. Stir in sour cream and mix until the mixture holds together. Stir in the cheese and jalapeño chillies. Shape into a ball. Cover and refrigerate overnight, or for at least six hours.

Preheat the oven to 190°C/375°F/Gas Mark 5. On a lightly floured board, roll out the dough into a quarter-inch thick rectangle. Cut into half-inch circles or any fancy shape with a cookie cutter. Place on an ungreased baking sheet, a few at a time. Bake in batches for 14 to 18 minutes until puffed and golden. Serve immediately.

Cheese-Olive Puffballs

INGREDIENTS

Makes 2 dozen puffballs

½ cup	plain flour
¼ tsp	baking powder
50 gms	butter
1 cup	grated Cheddar cheese
½ tsp	salt
1 tbsp	finely chopped parsley
12-14	stuffed olives

To serve

Mustard paste or Tabasco

METHOD

Sift the flour with the baking powder. Mix together butter, flour, cheese, salt and parsley. Place in a refrigerator to chill. Preheat the oven to 200°C/400°F/Gas Mark 6. Shape generous teaspoonsful of the chilled dough into balls. Press in the centre to make a deep depression, insert an olive and cover the olive with the dough. Bake in the oven for 15 minutes. Serve hot with mustard and Tabasco.

Chickpea and Potato Falafels

INGREDIENTS **Makes 24 falafels**

125 gms	chickpeas, soaked and boiled
1 medium	potato, boiled and peeled
2 tbsp	ginger-garlic paste
1 tsp	cumin powder
1 tsp	Zatar Mix (see below)
1 tsp	salt
2	green chillies, finely chopped
½ cup	shelled green peas, boiled
3 tbsp	plain flour
3 tbsp	cracked wheat (burghul)
2	spring onion stems, finely chopped

Oil for deep-frying

To serve

Tahina Sauce (recipe follows)

METHOD

Mash chickpeas and potatoes to a smooth paste. Add the rest of the ingredients, except the oil, and mix well. Form walnut-sized balls of the mixture and flatten them slightly. Cover and set aside for half an hour. Deep-fry in hot oil until golden brown. Serve with tahina sauce.

Tahina Sauce

Mix together 1 cup thick yogurt, 2 tbsp tahina paste, 1 chopped green chilli, 1 tbsp lemon juice, salt, sugar and mustard to taste.

Note: Zatar Mix is a mixture of ground thyme, sumac, sesame seeds and salt.

Cheese Loaf

INGREDIENTS

Serves 4-6

1 tbsp	unflavoured gelatine
¼ cup	Vegetable Stock (page 166)
2 cups	grated processed cheese
½ tsp	salt
½ tsp	pepper
½ tsp	mustard
½ tsp	dried mixed herbs
1 tbsp	vinegar
1 tbsp	olive oil
½ cup	chopped red pepper
½ cup	chopped walnuts, toasted
1 cup	whipped cream

To garnish

Freshly chopped herbs

To serve

Crackers or toasted bread

METHOD

Mix gelatine in vegetable stock and cook on low heat until dissolved. Remove from heat and set aside to cool. Mix together cheese, salt, pepper, mustard, herbs, vinegar and olive oil in a liquidiser jar and blend till smooth. With the blender working, pour the gelatine mixture in a thin stream and blend until smooth. Transfer to a mixing bowl and gently fold in the pepper, walnuts and cream. Pour the mixture into an oiled 6-inch x 3-inch x 2-inch loaf tin and freeze until set. Turn the loaf out onto a serving platter, garnish with the herbs and serve with crackers or toasted bread.

Note: This can be served as a moulded salad, surrounded by or on a bed of lettuce leaves.

Chilli Bean Curd

INGREDIENTS **Serves 4**

1 tbsp	plain flour
1 tbsp	cornflour
½ tsp	salt
200 gms	bean curd, cut into 1-inch pieces
2 tsp	oil + for deep-frying
2 tsp	butter
4-5	green chillies, slit lengthways
1 tbsp	crushed ginger
4-5 cloves	garlic, crushed
½ tsp	salt
½ tsp	pepper
½ tsp	sugar
2 tsp	soy sauce
1 tbsp	chilli sauce
½ tbsp	vinegar
2	spring onion stems, cut lengthways
1 tbsp	finely chopped coriander

A pinch of MSG (optional)

METHOD

Mix together the plain flour, cornflour and salt. Roll bean curd in the mixture and deep-fry in batches in hot oil till golden brown. Set aside. In a separate frying pan, heat two teaspoons of oil and butter together and fry the green chillies, ginger, and garlic. Add salt, pepper, sugar and MSG (if using). Add soy sauce, chilli sauce and vinegar and stir. Add a little water to prevent the mixture from sticking to the pan. Add bean curd, spring onions and coriander and mix well. Serve hot on toothpicks.

Note: You may use pieces of cottage cheese or vegetables like baby corn and mushrooms in place of the bean curd.

Chilli-Cheese Popcorn

INGREDIENTS **Serves 8**

2 tbsp	oil or shortening
1/3 cup	popcorn kernels
2 tbsp	butter
¼ tsp	garlic salt
¼ tsp	chilli powder
¼ cup	grated Cheddar cheese

METHOD

Pop the corn in hot oil in a pressure cooker. In a frying pan, heat butter and add garlic salt and chilli powder. Mix into the popcorn while still hot. Add the cheese and toss to coat. Serve immediately.

Chilli-Cheese Wrap-ups

INGREDIENTS **Makes 18 pieces**

1 cup	grated Cheddar cheese
2½ tbsp	butter
1 tbsp	chilli powder
1 tbsp	minced onion
1 tbsp	finely chopped green chillies
½ cup	plain flour
½ tbsp	milk

A pinch of salt

Filling

250 grams mixed ingredients (boiled baby potatoes, stuffed olives, halved walnuts, button mushrooms)

To serve

Chilli sauce and mustard paste

METHOD

Preheat the oven to 180°C/350°F/Gas Mark 4. Beat cheese, butter, chilli powder, minced onion and chillies in a bowl. Add the flour, milk and salt and make a soft dough. If the dough is too soft to handle, place it in a refrigerator for 5 minutes before rolling out into a ¼-inch thick rectangle. Cut into triangles, large enough to wrap around each of the filling ingredients. Wrap each filling ingredient individually with the dough triangles. Place on an ungreased baking sheet and bake for 10-12 minutes. Serve hot with chilli sauce and mustard.

Chilli-Mustard Potatoes

INGREDIENTS **Serves 4-6**

500 gms	baby potatoes, boiled and peeled
2 tbsp	mustard oil
½ tsp	cumin seeds
1 medium	onion, finely chopped
1	bay leaf
2 tbsp	ginger-garlic paste
½ tsp	chilli powder
½ tsp	cumin powder
1 tsp	garam masala
1 tsp	sugar
1 tbsp	mustard paste
1 tsp	lemon juice
1 cup	thick coconut milk
1 tsp	cornflour
2-3	green chillies, finely chopped

Salt to taste

To garnish

Chopped coriander

METHOD

Toss the potatoes in 1 tablespoon oil and place them on a hot grill till they turn slightly golden brown. Heat remaining oil in a round-bottomed pan till it begins to smoke. Add cumin seeds, onion and bay leaf and sauté for 1-2 minutes. Add ginger-garlic paste, chilli powder, cumin powder and garam masala and sauté till fragrant. Sprinkle a little water to prevent the spices from sticking. Add sugar to bring out the colour of the spices. Add potatoes, mustard paste, salt, lemon juice and coconut milk mixed with the cornflour. Cook till the potatoes are coated with the spices. Add green chillies just before removing from heat. Transfer to a serving plate, garnish with coriander and stick toothpicks on each potato. Serve at once.

Cocktail Puffed Breads
(Mini Parathas)

INGREDIENTS **Makes 12**

For the dough

1 cup	plain flour
¼ cup	wholewheat flour
¼ cup	semolina
2 tbsp	hot ghee

A pinch of salt
Oil for shallow-frying

For the filling

1 tbsp	oil
1 tsp	cumin seeds
4	green chillies, finely chopped
2 tbsp	finely chopped garlic
1 inch	ginger, finely grated
1 cup	green gram, soaked, cooked and ground to a paste
1 cup	grated cottage cheese
2 tsp	chaat masala
1 tsp	toasted sesame seeds
2 tbsp	finely chopped coriander

Salt to taste

To serve

Green Chutney (page 236) and sliced onions

METHOD

For the dough

Mix all the flours and salt. Make a well in the centre, pour in the hot ghee, cover and set aside for 10 minutes. Make a soft dough, cover and leave the dough to rest for half an hour.

For the filling

Heat the oil in a frying pan; sauté cumin seeds, green chillies, garlic and ginger. Add green gram paste and cottage cheese and cook for 3-4 minutes. Add chaat masala, sesame seeds, salt and coriander. Cook till the mixture is dry. Remove from heat and set aside to cool.

Divide the dough into 2 parts and roll each one out very thin. Cut into 3-inch rounds with a cutter, Place 1-2 tablespoons of the filling on each round and fold over to form a half-moon shape. Crimp the edges and seal. Shallow-fry the stuffed parathas in hot oil till golden brown. Serve with green chutney and sliced onions.

Chow-Chu Potatoes

INGREDIENTS **Serves 4**

250 gms	potatoes, peeled and cut into finger chips
2 tbsp	plain flour
2 tbsp	cornflour
3-4	green chillies, slit
1 tsp	coarsely ground rock salt

Oil for deep-frying

METHOD

Soak the potatoes in ice-cold water for one hour. Drain. Mix together the plain flour and cornflour. Roll each potato chip in the flour mixture and deep-fry in hot oil until crisp. Drain on kitchen paper and transfer to a serving plate. Lightly fry the chillies in a little oil and sprinkle coarse salt over them. Toss the fried potatoes with the chillies and serve hot.

Corn and Walnut Dip

INGREDIENTS **Makes 2 cups**

200 gms	cream cheese spread
½ tbsp	chilli flakes
½ tbsp	cumin powder
½ tsp	salt
½ tsp	pepper
1 tbsp	olive oil
1 tsp	lemon juice
1 cup	fresh or tinned corn kernels
½ cup	toasted chopped walnuts
1 small	onion, finely chopped

To serve

Tortilla chips or wafers

METHOD

Beat cream cheese with chilli flakes, cumin powder, salt, pepper, olive oil and lemon juice until smooth. Stir in corn, walnuts and onion. Transfer to a serving bowl, serve cold or at room temperature with tortilla chips or wafers.

Corn Chilli-Cheese Toast

INGREDIENTS **Serves 6**

1 tin (340 gms)	cream-style corn
½ cup	finely chopped boiled carrot
½ cup	mashed potato
1 tbsp	butter + for each slice of bread
5-6	spring onion stems, finely chopped
5-6	green chillies, finely chopped
12-14	bread slices
½ cup	grated Cheddar cheese

Salt and pepper to taste

To serve
Chilli sauce

METHOD

Mix together the corn, carrot, and mashed potato. Melt the butter in a frying pan and sauté spring onion stems and chillies for 4-5 minutes. Add the corn mixture along with salt and pepper. Remove from heat and set aside to cool. Add grated cheese and mix well. Preheat the oven to 170°C/325°F/Gas Mark 3. Spread the corn mixture evenly on the slices of bread. Dot each one with a little butter. Arrange on a baking sheet and bake for 20-25 minutes. Remove and cut each toast in 3 strips and serve immediately with chilli sauce.

Corn Kababs

INGREDIENTS **Makes 10-12 kababs**

1 tbsp	oil + for shallow-frying
½ medium	capsicum, finely chopped
1 medium	onion, grated
2 tbsp	ginger-chilli-garlic paste
1 tbsp	garam masala
2 cups	corn kernels, coarsely ground
1 tsp	lemon juice
1 tbsp	finely chopped fresh coriander
1 tbsp	cornflour

Salt to taste
Breadcrumbs to roll

To serve
Green Chutney (page 236)

METHOD

Heat oil in a frying pan; sauté capsicum, onion and ginger-chilli-garlic paste for 2-3 minutes. Add garam masala, salt and corn. Cook until the corn is soft. Remove from heat and add lemon juice, coriander and cornflour. Shape the mixture into cylindrical kababs. Roll in breadcrumbs and shallow-fry in oil in a non-stick frying pan till golden brown. Serve hot with green chutney.

Corn Manchurian

INGREDIENTS **Serves 6**

250 gms	grated corn kernels
150 gms	plain flour
1 tsp	baking powder
2 medium	carrots, peeled and grated
2	spring onion stems, finely chopped
2-3 cloves	garlic, crushed
1 medium	green capsicum, finely chopped
¼ cup	water
Salt to taste	
Oil for frying	

For the sauce

1 tbsp	oil
1 tbsp	finely chopped garlic
1 tbsp	finely chopped green chilli
1 tbsp	finely chopped red chilli
1 tbsp	finely chopped ginger
2	spring onion stems, finely chopped
2 tsp	soy sauce
1 cup	Vegetable Stock (page 166)
2 tbsp	cornflour mixed with ¼ cup water
½ tsp	salt
½ tsp	sugar
½ tsp	pepper
½ tsp	chilli sauce

METHOD

In a large bowl, mix all the ingredients except oil. Make walnut-sized balls and fry them in hot oil till golden brown.

For the sauce

Heat oil in a saucepan and fry garlic, green and red chillies, ginger and onion till soft. Add the remaining ingredients and bring to a boil, stirring continuously. Remove from heat when the mixture thickens.

To serve

Place the hot cornballs on a serving plate and pour the hot sauce over the balls. Stick toothpicks on each one and serve immediately.

Corn Salsa Tostadas

INGREDIENTS

Makes 18 tostadas

18	4-inch tortillas or small flat tacos
¾ cup	Sour Cream (page 234)
2	finely chopped spring onion stems
1 tbsp	finely chopped coriander
2 cloves	garlic, crushed
¾ cup	boiled yellow corn kernels
1 tbsp	finely chopped jalapeño chillies
1 medium	tomato, finely chopped
2 tbsp	orange juice
1 tsp	salad oil
Oil for brushing	
Taco seasoning	
Salt to taste	

METHOD

Brush the tortillas with oil and bake in a hot oven for four to five minutes or until crisp. Set aside to cool. If using flat tacos use them as they are. In a small bowl, combine the sour cream, spring onion, 1 teaspoon coriander and garlic. Cover and refrigerate.

To make the corn salsa

In a bowl, combine the corn, jalapeño chillies, tomato, orange juice, salad oil, taco seasoning, remaining coriander leaves and salt; cover and refrigerate. Just before serving, spread some sour cream mixture on each tostada and using a slotted spoon, top with a teaspoon of the corn salsa. Serve immediately.

Corn Snack
(Makai Bhel)

INGREDIENTS **Serves 4-6**

2 cups	boiled corn kernels
1 cup	boiled green peas
1 cup	boiled and cubed potatoes
2 medium	onions, finely chopped
2 medium	tomatoes, finely chopped
1 medium	green capsicum, finely chopped
1 medium	unripe green mango, finely chopped
½ cup	finely chopped coriander
½ cup	Sweet and Sour Chutney (page 236)
½ cup	Mint Chutney (page 236)

Salt, chilli powder and chaat masala to taste

To garnish
Fine sev and boondi

METHOD

In a large bowl, mix together corn, peas, potatoes, onions, tomatoes, capsicum and mango. Toss gently to mix and set aside. When ready to serve, add salt, chilli powder, chaat masala, coriander and the required amount of chutneys. Serve in individual bowls, garnished with sev, boondi and additional coriander. Serve additional chutney on the side.

Corn Toast with Parmesan Mayonnaise

INGREDIENTS

$1\frac{1}{2}$ cups	yellow corn kernels, boiled
1 tbsp	butter
$\frac{1}{2}$ cup	Mayonnaise (page 230)
$\frac{1}{2}$ cup	Parmesan cheese
$\frac{1}{2}$ cup	thick cream
2 cloves	garlic, crushed
2	spring onion stems, finely chopped
6-8	wholewheat or multigrain bread slices

Salt and pepper to taste

METHOD

Pack corn kernels in a piece of foil with butter. Place under a preheated grill for 5-10 minutes. In a small bowl, beat together the mayonnaise, cheese and cream until fluffy. Stir in the garlic, salt, pepper and spring onions. Toast the bread till crisp. Spread 2-3 tablespoons of grilled buttered corn kernels on each toast. Top with the mayonnaise mixture and place under a hot grill for 1 minute and serve.

Cottage Cheese, Pepper and Herb Sandwiches

INGREDIENTS

Makes 16 portions

¼ cup	butter
8	triangular or brown bread slices, crusts removed
1 cup	crumbled cottage cheese
¼ cup	Mayonnaise (page 230)
¼ cup	cream cheese
½ cup	finely chopped red pepper
½ cup	finely chopped onion
½ cup	finely chopped tomato
6-8	fresh basil, chopped

Salt, pepper and mustard to taste
A few lettuce leaves

METHOD

In a small bowl, mix together butter, salt, pepper and mustard. Lightly butter the bread slices. Cover with a damp cloth and set aside. In another bowl, beat the cottage cheese, mayonnaise and cream cheese until light and fluffy. Stir in the red pepper, onion, tomato and basil. Place each slice of bread on a cutting board and spread with 3-4 tablespoons of the cottage cheese mixture. Cover with a few lettuce leaves and then with another slice of bread. Cut each sandwich into four triangles and serve. Alternatively, grill the whole sandwich and cut into bite-size pieces.

Courgette, Carrot and Feta Cheese Fritters

INGREDIENTS

2 large	carrots, peeled and grated
2 large	courgettes, peeled and grated
1 small	onion, grated
¼ cup	crumbled feta cheese
¼ cup	plain flour
1 tsp	baking powder
½ tsp	cumin seeds
½ tsp	poppy seeds
1 tsp	curry powder
1 tbsp	finely chopped fresh parsley
1 tbsp	finely chopped fresh basil
¼ cup	tomato purée
2-3 tbsp	butter
2-3 tbsp	oil

Salt and pepper to taste

To serve

Yogurt-Mint Sauce (recipe below)

METHOD

Mix together carrots, courgettes, onion and feta cheese in a bowl. In another bowl, mix together flour, baking powder, cumin and poppy seeds, curry powder, parsley, basil, salt and pepper. Toss the carrot mixture with the flour mixture until well combined. Stir in the tomato purée and mix well. Heat the butter and oil in a large frying pan. Place heaped tablespoons of the carrot-flour mixture in the pan, flattening them slightly with the back of a spoon. Fry gently for about 2 minutes on each side till golden brown and crisp. Drain on paper towels. Serve warm with yogurt-mint sauce.

Yogurt-Mint Sauce

In a bowl, combine 1 cup beaten yogurt with 2 tbsp finely chopped mint, ½ tsp salt, ½ tsp sugar and ½ tsp lemon juice. Place in a refrigerator to chill.

Creamed Corn Fondue

INGREDIENTS — **Serves 6-8**

2 tbsp	butter
¼ cup	finely chopped onion
2 tbsp	finely chopped green capsicum
1 tin (400 gms)	cream-style corn
2 tbsp	cornflour, mixed with ¼ cup water
1½ cups	grated Cheddar cheese
1 tsp	Worcestershire sauce
1 tsp	vinegar

Salt and pepper to taste

To garnish
Green chillies in vinegar

To serve
Crisp fried wontons

METHOD

Melt the butter in a fondue dish over medium heat. Add the chopped onion and capsicum and cook until soft. Add creamed corn and cornflour mixture and stir well. Continue to cook until thick. Add the grated cheese, half a cup at a time, stirring after each addition. Add salt, pepper, Worcestershire sauce and vinegar. Mix well, drizzle chillies in vinegar on top and serve hot with crisp fried wontons.

Note: If you feel that the mixture is too thick, add 2-3 tablespoons of vegetable stock.

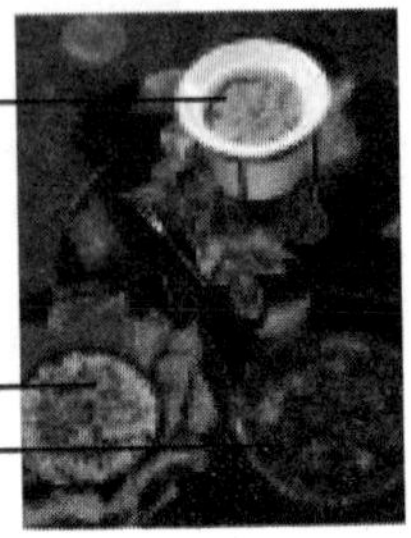

Creamed Corn Fondue
Corn and Walnut Dip
Chilli-Mustard Potatoes

Curried Mushrooms

INGREDIENTS **Serves 4**

3-4 tbsp	oil
1 large	onion, grated
3-4 cloves	garlic, crushed
2 tsp	pav-bhaji masala powder
1 tsp	chilli powder (optional)
250 gms	fresh button mushrooms, stemmed, washed and halved
2 medium	tomatoes, grated
2 tbsp	finely chopped coriander
Salt to taste	

METHOD

Heat the oil in a frying pan; fry the onion and garlic till soft. Add pav-bhaji masala and chilli powder and fry for 2-3 minutes. When the oil separates, add the mushrooms. Cook until the mushrooms are soft but firm. Add the tomatoes and salt. Cook till all the liquid evaporates. Turn out onto a serving plate, sprinkle coriander leaves and serve with toothpicks.

Creamy Pizza Fondue

INGREDIENTS **Serves 6-8**

1 tbsp	olive oil
1-2 tsp	finely chopped garlic
2 tsp	dried oregano
2 cups	Marinara Sauce (page 232)
3 cups	mixed grated mozzarella and Cheddar cheese
1 tbsp	cornflour
½ cup	pizza toppings of your choice (green pepper, onion, olive, etc.)
½ cup	cream
5-6	basil leaves, finely chopped
1-2 tbsp	Vegetable Stock (page 166)

Salt, pepper and chilli flakes to taste

To serve

Crusty bread or foccacia cubes, or cooked pasta shapes such as penne

METHOD

In a small pan, heat oil and fry garlic and oregano for 1 minute. Add the marinara sauce and cook for 1 minute. Toss cheese in a mixture of cornflour, salt, pepper and chilli flakes. Add the cheese a little by little and keep mixing till melted and all the cheese is incorporated. Add the pizza toppings of your choice, cream and basil leaves and mix well. If the mixture is too thick, add a little stock. Serve in a fondue pot over a burner with bread cubes, foccacia cubes or cooked pasta shapes.

Crispy Corn Kernels

INGREDIENTS **Serves 4**

1 cup	yellow corn kernels, boiled
½	egg, slightly beaten or 1-2 tsp water
1 tbsp	cornflour
2 tbsp	plain flour
2 tsp	soy sauce
¼ tsp	chilli powder
2-3 cloves	garlic, minced

A pinch of MSG (optional)
Salt to taste
Oil for deep-frying

METHOD

Coat the corn kernels with beaten egg or water. In another small bowl, mix together the rest of the ingredients, except oil. Rub all the dry ingredients over the corn kernels. Heat oil and fry corn in three or four batches making sure that all the kernels remain separate. Serve hot as a starter.

Crispy Rice with Vegetables

INGREDIENTS

Serves 4

1 tbsp oil
1 tbsp red chilli paste
1 tbsp garlic paste
¼ cup finely chopped carrot
¼ cup finely chopped onion
¼ cup finely chopped bean sprouts
¼ cup finely chopped French beans
½ tsp pepper
1 tbsp soy sauce
1 tsp vinegar
1 tsp sugar
1 cup Fried noodles (recipe follows)
2 cups Crispy Rice (recipe follows)
A pinch of MSG (optional)
Salt to taste

To garnish

1 tbsp finely chopped coriander

To serve

Chilli sauce

METHOD

Heat oil in a frying pan; fry chilli and garlic pastes for a few seconds. Add the vegetables, MSG (if using), salt, pepper, soy sauce, vinegar and sugar. Cook until the vegetables are soft. When ready to serve, add the noodles and rice. Toss gently to mix well. Garnish with coriander and serve.

Crispy Rice **Makes 1½-2 cups**

Wash and drain 1 cup rice. Cook in plenty of water until almost done. Drain and spread on a tray lined with a piece of muslin. Cover and dry in the sun until the rice is crisp. Store in an ai ht jar and use as required.

Fried oodles **Makes 1 cup**

Blanch cup fresh or dried noodles in hot water for 3-4 minutes. Drain completely and deep-fr n hot oil. Drain on kitchen paper.

Crumb-fried Potato Wedges

INGREDIENTS Serves 4

½ cup	water
2-3 tbsp	plain flour
1 large	onion, finely chopped
2-3	green chillies, finely chopped
250 gms	potatoes, parboiled and cut into wedges
1 cup	breadcrumbs

Salt and pepper to taste
Oil for deep-frying

To serve
Red Salsa (page 234) or Sour Cream (page 234)

METHOD

Mix together water, flour, onion, chillies, salt and pepper in a bowl. Roll each potato wedge in the mixture until thickly coated. Roll in breadcrumbs and deep-fry in hot oil. Drain on paper towels and serve with salsa or sour cream.

Cucumber Mousse

INGREDIENTS **Serves 4**

300 gms	silken tofu
1 cup	crumbled cottage cheese
1 tbsp	unflavoured gelatine
1 large	cucumber, peeled and finely chopped
3	spring onion stems, finely chopped
1 tbsp	finely chopped chives or mint
½ cup	thick cream, beaten

Salt and pepper to taste

To serve

Crackers

METHOD

Process tofu and cottage cheese together in a blender until smooth. Mix gelatine with ¼ cup water and heat on low heat till melted. Pour the melted gelatine over the tofu-cottage cheese mixture and blend again until smooth. Transfer to a bowl and stir in the cucumber, spring onions and chives or mint, salt and pepper. Fold in the beaten cream and mix well. Pour into individual ramekins or stemmed glasses and chill for 2-3 hours. Serve with crackers.

Curd Cheese with Lavash

INGREDIENTS

Serves 4

½ cup cottage cheese
1 cup thick yogurt
Salt to taste
Green or black olives

For the herb sauce

1 tbsp chopped chives
1 tbsp chopped basil
1 tbsp chopped parsley
2 tbsp olive oil
1 clove garlic, crushed
Salt and pepper to taste

To serve

Crisp lavash bread

METHOD

Blend together cottage cheese, yogurt and salt until smooth. Pour into a metal bowl and leave to set in a refrigerator overnight.

For the herb sauce

Blend all the ingredients till smooth and pour into a shallow serving dish.

Scoop out small balls of the set cheese mixture with a melon-baller and arrange them in the sauce along with the olives. Serve with crisp lavash bread.

Creamy Dijon-topped Potatoes

INGREDIENTS **Makes 24 portions**

200 gms	cream cheese, softened
¼ cup	Dijon mustard
1 tbsp	chopped fresh basil
1/3 cup	finely chopped black olives
¼ cup	finely chopped spring onion
¼ cup	finely chopped red pepper
10-12	small potatoes, roasted and cut lengthways in half

To garnish

Spring onion tips

METHOD

In a medium bowl, with an electric mixer at medium speed, beat cream cheese, mustard and basil until smooth. Stir in olives, spring onions and red pepper. To serve, pipe or spoon 1 tablespoon of the mixture onto each potato half and garnish with spring onion tips.

Curried Vegetable Quesadillas

INGREDIENTS **Serves 6-8**

1 cup	thinly shredded cabbage
½ cup	finely chopped onion
½ cup	finely chopped carrot
1 tbsp	ginger-garlic paste
1 tbsp	curry powder
1 tbsp	oil
1 cup	mashed potato
¼ cup	boiled green peas
1 tbsp	lemon juice
1 tbsp	chopped coriander
8	6-inch flour tortillas
1 cup	grated processed or Monterey Jack cheese

Salt to taste
Oil to brush tortillas

To serve
Red Chilli Jam (recipe follows)

METHOD

Preheat the oven to 180°C/350°F/Gas Mark 4. Sauté the cabbage, onion, carrot, ginger-garlic paste and curry powder in the oil. Cook over medium heat until vegetables are tender, but crisp. Remove from heat and add the mashed potato, peas, salt, lemon juice and coriander. Set aside to cool. Place four tortillas on baking sheets. Spread half a cup of vegetable mixture on each tortilla; top with a quarter cup of cheese and cover with another tortilla. Press gently to seal the edges of both tortillas. Brush with a little oil and bake for fifteen minutes, or till thoroughly heated. Cut each quesadilla into four wedges and serve with red chilli jam.

Red Chilli Jam **Makes 3/4 cup**

Heat 2 tbsp oil in a small saucepan; fry 1 tbsp ginger-garlic paste for 1 minute. Add ½ cup finely chopped dried red chillies and cook for 2-3 minutes. Add ¼ cup sugar, a pinch of salt and 2 tbsp vinegar. Cook until sugar has melted and is of a syrupy consistency. Remove from heat and cool.

Delightful Herb Spread

INGREDIENTS **Makes $1\frac{1}{2}$ cups**

200 gms cream cheese
2 tbsp thick cream
2 tbsp butter
2 cloves garlic, crushed
1 tbsp freshly chopped parsley
2 tsp freshly chopped chives
2 tsp freshly chopped chervil
$\frac{1}{4}$ tsp lemon juice
$\frac{1}{4}$ tsp pepper
Salt to taste

To serve
Assorted crackers or crusty bread

METHOD

Bring the cream cheese, cream and butter to room temperature. In a mixing bowl, beat the cream cheese, cream and butter with a mixer at medium speed until the ingredients are mixed well. Beat in the garlic, parsley, chives, chervil, lemon juice, salt and pepper until well blended. Cover with cling film and chill overnight or at least 3-4 hours. Serve with crackers or crusty bread.

Devilled Peas in Toast Cups

INGREDIENTS **Serves 10**

3 tbsp	chopped onion
3 tbsp	chopped green capsicum
1 tbsp	butter
2 tbsp	mushroom or vegetable soup powder
½ cup	shelled and boiled green peas
3 tbsp	chopped red pepper
8-10	slices wholewheat bread, crusts removed
2-3	cheese slices

Salt, pepper and chilli flakes to taste

METHOD

Preheat the oven to 180°C/350°F/Gas Mark 4. Sauté onion and capsicum in butter until tender. Remove from heat. Mix the soup powder with 3 tablespoons hot water. Stir in the soup mixture, peas, red pepper, salt, pepper and chilli flakes. Moisten the bread slices and press into cupcake moulds. Bake for 20 minutes, till golden brown. Take out of the oven and remove the toast cups from the moulds. Fill with the pea mixture. Cut each cheese slice into 4 pieces and place a piece on top of the pea mixture in each toast cup. Bake again for 3-4 minutes till the cheese melts. Serve immediately.

Egyptian Spice Blend
(Dukkah)

INGREDIENTS **Makes 1½ cups**

2/3 cup	hazelnuts
½ cup	sesame seeds
2 tbsp	coriander seeds
2 tbsp	cumin seeds
1 tsp	sea salt or rock salt
2 tbsp	black pepper

To serve
Toasted crusty bread and olive oil

METHOD

Preheat the oven to 180°C/350°F/Gas Mark 4. Place hazelnuts on a baking sheet and bake for about 5 minutes. Remove and set aside to cool. In a dry frying pan, roast sesame seeds over medium heat until light golden brown. Remove and transfer to a bowl. In the same pan, roast coriander and cumin seeds until they begin to pop. Grind to a fine powder. Add to the sesame seeds. Place the cooled hazelnuts in a food processor or grinder, and process until finely ground. Stir into the bowl with the spices. Add salt and pepper and mix well.

To serve
Serve with toasted crusty bread and olive oil. Dip bread into the olive oil, then into the dukkah.

Fenugreek Millet Cookies
(Methi Bajri ni Puri)

Makes 18-20 puris

INGREDIENTS

½ cup	fenugreek leaves
1 cup	millet flour
1 tsp	oil + for greasing
1 tsp	black pepper
1 tsp	garlic
1 tsp	sesame seeds
1 tsp	ginger-chilli paste
½ tsp	turmeric powder

Plain flour for dusting
Salt to taste

To serve
Green Chutney (page 236) or yogurt

METHOD

Preheat the oven to 150°C/300°F/Gas Mark 2. Chop fenugreek leaves, sprinkle half a teaspoon salt and set aside. Mix together millet flour, 1 teaspoon oil, salt, pepper, garlic, sesame seeds, ginger-chilli paste and turmeric. Mix fenugreek leaves with the flour mixture and make a moderately soft dough with water. Divide the dough into small cherry-sized balls. Take one ball at a time, place it on a floured surface and flatten with your palm into large coin-sized discs (puris). Prick with a sharp knife or fork. Arrange on a greased baking tray and bake for 15 minutes until crisp. Store in an airtight container. Serve with chutney or yogurt as a teatime snack.

Feta Cheese Cigars

INGREDIENTS

Makes 12-14 portions

2 cups	spinach leaves
1 tbsp	butter
1 tbsp	plain flour
1 cup	crumbled feta cheese
¼ cup	finely chopped walnuts or pine nuts
12-14	wonton wrappers or squares of phyllo pastry

Salt, pepper and nutmeg to taste
Melted butter to brush the pastry

METHOD

Boil and purée the spinach leaves. In a small pan, melt the butter, add the flour and cook for 1 minute. Add puréed spinach, salt, pepper and nutmeg. Cook until all the water dries up. Remove from heat and set aside to cool. Mix in the crumbled feta cheese and nuts.

Preheat the oven to 190°C/375°F/Gas Mark 5. Place each wonton wrapper on a board and brush lightly with melted butter. Spoon 1 tablespoon of spinach mixture in the centre. Lift up one corner of the wrapper and roll up towards the opposite corner. Press lightly to seal. Twist the roll into a half-moon shape. Place all the pastries on a baking sheet. Brush with melted butter and bake for 15-20 minutes or until golden brown. Serve hot.

Fresh Green Pea Hummus

INGREDIENTS **Serves 6-8**

2 cups	shelled green peas
¼ cup	tahina
½ cup	finely chopped coriander leaves
2 cloves	garlic
1 tsp	salt
½ tsp	pepper
½ tsp	roasted cumin powder
2-3 tbsp	lemon juice

For the pita toasts

2	7-inch pita breads
1 large clove	garlic, crushed with a little salt
2 tbsp	olive oil

To garnish

A dash of olive oil
1 sprig of coriander

METHOD

For the pita toasts

Preheat the oven to 190°C/375°F/Gas Mark 5. Cut each pita bread in half. Soak the garlic in olive oil. Brush the garlic oil on each pita half. Arrange the bread in one layer on a baking sheet and bake until toasted. Cut into triangles and set aside to cool.

Cook peas in a saucepan in boiling salted water until just tender. Drain and cool. In a liquidiser jar or food processor, process the peas, tahina, coriander, garlic, salt, pepper, cumin powder and lemon juice to make a smooth purée. Transfer to a serving bowl, garnish with olive oil and a sprig of coriander and serve with toasted pita bread.

Garden Vegetable Pizza

INGREDIENTS **Makes 24 appetisers**

4	6-inch wholewheat pizza bases
2 tbsp	olive oil
½ cup	whipping cream
1 cup	cream cheese
1 tbsp	vinegar
1 tsp	Italian seasoning
1 tsp	chilli flakes
2-3	fresh basil leaves, chopped
½ cup	blanched broccoli
½ cup	chopped capsicum
½ cup	chopped tomato
¼ cup	chopped onion
¼ cup	chopped lettuce
¼ cup	chopped olives

Salt and pepper to taste

METHOD

Preheat the oven to 180°C/350°F/Gas Mark 4. Trim the pizza bases and brush them with 1 tablespoon olive oil. Bake for 10-12 minutes or until golden brown. Remove and set aside to cool. Whip the cream in a small bowl until stiff. In a separate bowl, combine cream cheese, whipped cream, vinegar, 1 tablespoon olive oil, Italian seasoning mix, chilli flakes, basil, salt and pepper. Spread the mixture evenly on the baked pizza bases. Pile all the vegetables on top and place in a refrigerator to chill. Cut into wedges and serve.

Gazpacho Sandwiches

INGREDIENTS **Serves 6**

1 medium	cucumber, deseeded and chopped
½ cup	black beans, soaked, cooked and drained
100 gms	feta cheese, cut into small cubes
¼ cup	finely chopped coriander
2 tbsp	cider vinegar
1 tbsp	olive oil
1 tbsp	chopped jalapeño chillies
1 large clove	garlic, chopped fine
1 tsp	paprika
3 large	tomatoes, halved
1 large	onion, cut into ½-inch thick slices
12-14	crusty bread slices, slightly toasted

Salt and pepper to taste

METHOD

In a medium-sized bowl, combine cucumber, beans, cheese, coriander, vinegar, olive oil, jalapeño chillies, garlic, paprika, salt and pepper. Set aside. Place tomatoes and onions under a hot grill until slightly charred. Remove and chop roughly. Add to cucumber mixture and toss gently to mix. Spoon the mixture onto toasted bread slices and serve.

Greek Eggplant Dip
(Muttabal)

INGREDIENTS

Serves 4-6

2 medium	eggplants, roasted
3 medium	tomatoes, coarsely chopped
2 cloves	garlic, finely chopped
1 tbsp	finely chopped parsley
1 medium	onion, finely chopped
1 tsp	salt
1 tsp	sugar
¼ tsp	pepper

Juice of 1 lemon

To garnish

Olive oil and red chilli powder

To serve

Crisp pita triangles

METHOD

Hold the roasted eggplants under running cold water and remove the skin. Place the eggplants on a board and chop coarsely. Transfer to a serving bowl. Add the rest of the ingredients. Make designs on the surface with a fork, drizzle olive oil and sprinkle chilli powder. Serve cold or at room temperature with crisp pita triangles.

Green Cottage Cheese Wraps
(Hara Paneer Kathi Rolls)

INGREDIENTS | **Serves 4**

500 gms	cottage cheese, cut into strips
2 tbsp	oil
2 medium	onions, sliced
2 medium	tomatoes, finely chopped
4 large	Roomali Rotis (recipe follows)

A few pieces of charcoal
Salt to taste

For the marinade

1 cup	chopped spinach leaves
½ cup	chopped mint
½ cup	chopped coriander
1 inch	ginger, chopped
1 tbsp	chopped green garlic
3-4	green chillies, chopped
1 tbsp	lemon juice
1 tbsp	oil
2 tbsp	roasted and powdered peanuts
1 tsp	chaat masala
1 tsp	black pepper powder
½ cup	grated coconut

Salt to taste

To serve

Green Chutney (page 236) mixed with yogurt.

METHOD

For the marinade, place all the ingredients in a blender and blend until smooth. In a shallow dish, place cottage cheese strips and pour the marinade mixture over. Set aside to marinate for 2 hours. In a thick-bottomed frying pan, heat oil, reserving 1 teaspoon. Add the cottage cheese along with the marinade and cook until all the liquid evaporates, stirring from time to time. If the mixture sticks to the sides, add a little water. Push all the mixture to the sides of the pan. Place the burning charcoal in a small metal bowl and place it in the centre of the pan. Pour the reserved teaspoon of oil over the charcoal and immediately cover the pan tightly with the lid. Keep covered until the coal stops smoking. Remove the lid and add the onions and the tomatoes and mix. Adjust the salt. Cook briefly till the vegetables wilt slightly. Remove from heat and keep warm.

To assemble the wrap, place one roti on a flat surface, spoon 2-3 tablespoons of the cottage cheese mixture in the centre and roll the roti up tightly. With a sharp knife, cut each roti diagonally into 3-4 pieces or serve whole. Serve with green chutney mixed with yogurt.

Roomali Roti

Make a dough with 1 cup plain flour, ½ tsp salt, 1 tbsp oil and 1/3 cup warm water. Cover and set aside for 45 minutes. Knead again and divide into 3 parts. Roll out each part into a paper-thin roti. Invert a heavy cast iron pan over a gas flame and spread the roti on it. Cook for 45 to 50 seconds. Remove, use immediately or fold into a triangle and cover with a piece of muslin.

Green Gram and Cottage Cheese Rolls
(Hara Bhara Moong Chilla)

INGREDIENTS

Serves 4-6

250 gms	split green gram, soaked for 4 hours
1 tbsp	crushed green chillies
1 tbsp	ginger
1 tbsp	finely chopped coriander
200 gms	grated cottage cheese
½ cup	finely chopped capsicum
½ cup	finely chopped tomato
½ cup	finely chopped onion

Salt to taste
Oil for cooking

To serve
Green Chutney (page 236) or Coconut Chutney (page 236)

METHOD

Grind the soaked gram to a fine paste with green chillies, ginger and coriander. Add salt. Mix cottage cheese, capsicum, tomato and onion in a small bowl. Heat a thick griddle and brush it with oil. Take a spoonful of the gram mixture and spread it on the hot griddle, as thinly as possible. Sprinkle 1 teaspoon of cottage cheese mixture all over. Drizzle a little oil around the edge of the pancake. Loosen it with a sharp spatula and roll it up like a flute. Pierce a toothpick through so that the roll does not open up. Serve hot with chutney.

Green Gram Cake
(Moong na Dhokla)

INGREDIENTS

Makes 14-16

1 cup	whole green gram, soaked for 6 hours
1 tbsp	finely chopped coriander
1 tbsp	ginger-chilli paste
1 tbsp	oil + for greasing
1 tsp	fruit salt

Juice of ½ lemon
Salt to taste

For the tempering

2 tbsp	oil
½ tsp	mustard seeds
4-5	curry leaves

A pinch of asafoetida

To garnish

3-4 tbsp finely chopped coriander and grated coconut

To serve

Green Chutney (page 236)

METHOD

Grind the green gram along with coriander leaves and water to a coarse paste. The batter should not be too thick or too thin. Place a metal ring at the bottom of a large vessel, add some water and bring to a boil. Grease a rimmed stainless steel plate with oil and place it on the ring in the boiling water.

For the dhokla, mix together green gram paste, ginger-chilli paste, salt, 1 tablespoon oil and fruit salt mixed with lemon juice. Mix the batter lightly in circular movements, till all the ingredients are completely incorporated. Immediately pour the batter into the greased plate over hot water. Cover tightly and steam for 15 minutes. Remove from the pan and set aside to cool slightly.

For the tempering

In a small vessel, heat oil; add mustard seeds and when they splutter, add asafoetida and curry leaves.

Pour over the steamed dhokla. Garnish with coriander and grated coconut and serve hot with green chutney.

Dips Platter

Cucumber and Mint Dip

Serves 4-6

INGREDIENTS

1 cup cream cheese
2 tbsp finely chopped onion
2 tbsp finely chopped mint
½ cup finely chopped cucumber
¼ cup whipping cream
Salt to taste

To garnish

Mint leaves and thin slices of unpeeled cucumber

To serve

Crisp pita chips

METHOD

Serves 4-6

Combine cream cheese, onion, mint, cucumber and salt. Fold in the whipped cream and pour the mixture into a serving bowl. Garnish with mint and sliced cucumber. Cover with cling film and chill. Serve with crisp pita chips.

Pepper and Sun-dried Tomato Dip

INGREDIENTS

½ cup cream cheese spread
½ cup cottage cheese
1 tbsp Mayonnaise (page 230)
1 tsp balsamic vinegar
1 tsp sugar
1 tbsp chopped garlic
1 tsp mustard paste
1 tsp olive oil
1 tbsp chopped basil
¼ cup finely chopped red pepper
¼ cup finely chopped sun-dried tomatoes
Salt and pepper to taste

To serve

Crackers and wafers

METHOD

Beat cream cheese, cottage cheese and mayonnaise together until creamy. Add balsamic vinegar, sugar, garlic, mustard paste, olive oil, basil, salt and pepper. Gently fold in the red pepper and sun-dried tomatoes. Pour the mixture into a serving bowl, cover with cling film and chill. Serve with crackers or wafers.

Garden Vegetable Dip

INGREDIENTS **Serves 4-6**

½ cup	thick yogurt
½ cup	whipping cream
2 cloves	garlic, crushed
1 tsp	chopped fresh parsley
1 tsp	chopped fresh chives
1 tsp	salt
1 tsp	mustard paste
1 tsp	lemon juice
1 tbsp	finely chopped carrots
1 tbsp	finely chopped cucumber
1 tbsp	finely chopped spring onions
1 tbsp	finely chopped green or red pepper
1 tbsp	finely chopped tomato

To serve

Pita crisps or crackers

METHOD

Blend yogurt, cream, garlic, parsley and chives in a blender untill smooth. Pour into a bowl and add salt, mustard paste and lemon juice. Fold in all the vegetables. Pour the mixture into a serving bowl, cover with cling film and chill. Serve with crackers or pita crisps.

Serving suggestion for dips and crisps :

Take a large platter; place 3 dips in 3 similar bowls. Surround them with dippers and in between, place vegetable sticks (crudités), and bunches of fresh herbs.

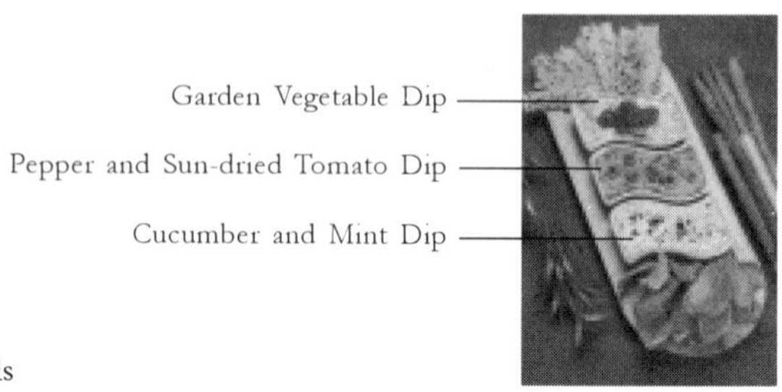

STAINLESS CHINA

Herbed Nuts

INGREDIENTS **Makes 1 cup**

1 cup	hazelnuts, toasted
2 tbsp	butter
1/4 tsp	dried oregano
1/4 tsp	thyme
1/4 tsp	chilli flakes

A pinch of cumin powder
Salt and pepper to taste

METHOD

Chop nuts coarsely. In a frying pan, melt butter. Add the rest of the ingredients and sauté until the nuts are well coated with the spices. Remove from heat and set aside to cool. Store in an airtight container.

Note: You can use any nuts in place of hazelnuts.

Jalapeños Rellenos
Herbed Nuts
Hot Dip Damper

Green Gram Snack
(Hara-Bhara Chaat)

INGREDIENTS **Makes 12 portions**

1 tbsp	oil
½ tsp	cumin seeds
1-2	green chillies, slit
250 gms	fresh green grams
250 gms	shelled green peas
1 tbsp	dried mango powder
¼ cup	Mint Chutney (page 236)
1 medium	tomato, finely chopped
1 medium	onion, finely chopped
1 tbsp	finely chopped coriander
1 tbsp	finely chopped green chillies

A few curry leaves
A pinch of soda bicarbonate
Black salt and salt to taste
Lemon juice to taste

To serve
Potato baskets or tart cases

To garnish
100 gms spinach sev

METHOD

Heat oil in a saucepan and fry the cumin seeds, green chillies and curry leaves. Add green gram and peas with a pinch of soda bicarbonate. Sprinkle a little water so that the mixture does not stick to the pan. Cook, uncovered, till soft. Stir in black salt, salt and mango powder. Just before serving, add mint chutney, chopped tomato, onion, coriander, chopped green chillies and lemon juice to the green gram mixtured and mix well. Spoon the mixture into potato baskets or tart cases, garnish with spinach sev and serve.

Grilled Mushrooms with Herbed Cheese

INGREDIENTS | **Serves 6-8**

12-14	mushrooms, stalks removed and washed
2 tbsp	olive oil
2 tbsp	breadcrumbs
3 tbsp	toasted and chopped walnuts or pine nuts
For the herbed cheese	
225 gms	cream cheese
2 cloves	garlic, crushed with a little salt
1 tbsp	chopped fresh mixed herbs
75 gms	butter, melted

METHOD

For the mushrooms

Clean the mushroom caps on the inside and remove the black parts. Brush with olive oil, sprinkle some breadcrumbs and place under a hot grill for 10-12 minutes or until soft but firm. Remove and set aside.

For the herbed cheese

In a bowl, beat cream cheese with the crushed garlic and fresh herbs. Gently fold the cooled melted butter into the mixture. Do not add the butter while hot or the mixture will curdle. Fill the mixture into a piping bag and pipe some of the mixture into the grilled mushrooms. Top with nuts and serve warm or cold.

Note: You can use this cheese mixture as a topping or stuffing for any vegetable such as cucumbers, tomatoes, peppers etc.

Harvest Party Mix

INGREDIENTS **Makes 5 cups**

¼ cup	butter
1 tsp	garlic salt
1 tsp	mixed dried herbs
1 tsp	Worcestershire sauce
1 cup	rice cereal
1 cup	bread sticks, cut into 1-inch pieces
1 cup	cheeselings
1 cup	salted peanuts without skin
1 cup	packaged potato straws
2-3 tbsp	grated Parmesan cheese (optional)

METHOD

Melt butter in a heavy saucepan. Add garlic salt, herbs and Worcestershire sauce. Add the remaining ingredients and toss gently to mix. Set aside to cool. Store in an airtight container

Green Gram Pasties
(Boote ke Samose)

INGREDIENTS

Makes 8 pasties

250 gms	plain flour
1 tbsp	oil + for binding the dough
6-8	green chillies, coarsely chopped
500 gms	shelled green gram, coarsely ground
2 tbsp	finely chopped coriander

Salt to taste
Juice of 2 lemons
Oil for deep-frying

To serve

Green Chutney (page 236)

METHOD

Make a moderately soft dough with plain flour, oil and water. Cover and set aside. Heat 1 tablespoon of oil in a frying pan and fry chillies for 2 minutes. Add a little water if necessary. Cook for 3-4 minutes. Add green gram, salt and a little more water. Cook until gram is tender and the mixture is dry. Stir in the lemon juice and coriander. Set aside to cool.

Divide the dough into 8 portions. Shape each portion into a ball. Roll out the dough to a 4-5 inch round. Cut the round in half. Fold each half to form a cone, sticking the ends with a little water. Stuff 1 tablespoon of mixture into the cone and seal the edges with a little water. Deep-fry in hot oil till crisp. Serve hot with green chutney.

Herb-Pepper Crisps with Spring Dip

INGREDIENTS **Serves 4-6**

4	7-inch round thin pizza bases
2 tbsp	melted butter
4 tbsp	Herb-Pepper Seasoning (recipe follows)
1 tbsp	finely chopped chives
For the dip	
1½ cups	crumbled cottage cheese
¼ cup	fresh cream, whisked
¼ cup	finely chopped spring onion
¼ cup	finely chopped capsicum
1 tsp	crushed garlic
1 tbsp	wine vinegar
1 tbsp	finely chopped fresh herbs (parsley, basil, thyme and tarragon)

Salt and pepper to taste

METHOD

Brush pizza bases with butter and sprinkle herb-pepper seasoning and chives. Cut each one into triangles and bake in a preheated oven at 180°C/350°F/Gas Mark 4 for 5-10 minutes till crisp. Remove and set aside to cool.

For the dip

Beat the cottage cheese and cream together in a bowl. Fold in the rest of the ingredients. Spoon the mixture into a serving bowl and chill in a refrigerator for half an hour or more.

Herb-Pepper Seasoning **Makes 4 tablespoons**

Mix together 2 tbsp dried mixed herbs, 2 tsp each salt and pepper, 1 tsp grated lemon rind and 1 tsp garlic powder.

Hot Asparagus Dip

INGREDIENTS **Makes 2 cups**

¼ cup	fresh cream
½ tsp	mustard powder
1 tsp	crushed garlic
1½ cups	fresh asparagus, cut into ½-inch pieces and blanched
1 cup	blanched and diced tomatoes
¼ cup	finely chopped spring onions
1 tbsp	finely chopped parsley
½ cup	cream cheese, softened

Salt and pepper to taste

To serve

Crackers or bread sticks

METHOD

Preheat the oven to 180°C/350°F/Gas Mark 4. Mix cream, salt, pepper, mustard and garlic. Arrange the rest of the ingredients in layers in a medium-sized greased baking dish. Pour the cream mixture over and bake for 30 minutes, or until hot and bubbly. Serve with crackers or bread sticks.

Hot Dip Damper

INGREDIENTS **Serves 6**

1 medium	onion, diced
2-3 cloves	garlic, crushed
1 tbsp	butter
1 medium	tomato, diced
1-2 tsp	curry powder
1½ cups	Sour Cream (page 234)
2 cups	grated processed cheese
1 round	loaf of bread

To serve
Crusty bread or crudités (cut raw vegetables)

METHOD

Preheat the oven to 180°C/350°F/Gas Mark 4. In a pan, fry the onion and garlic in butter until soft. Add tomato and curry powder and cook for another minute. Remove from heat and set aside to cool. In a large bowl, mix together sour cream, grated cheese and the onion mixture. Slice off the top of the loaf and scoop out the inside to hollow it out. Toast the hollowed bread in the oven for 5 minutes. Pour the prepared mixture into the hollowed loaf. Place on a tray and bake for 20-25 minutes. Chop the scooped out bread into pieces, and place in the oven till crisp. Serve the hot dip with the crisp bread, crusty bread or crudités.

Hot Mexican Corn Fajitas

INGREDIENTS **Makes 12 fajitas**

1/3 cup	Mayonnaise (page 230)
½ cup	grated Cheddar cheese
½ cup	Sour Cream (page 234)
1 cup	corn kernels, boiled
¼ cup	finely chopped jalapeño chillies
2-3	spring onion stems, finely chopped
1 tsp	taco seasoning
12 small	(3-4 inch) tortillas

Salt to taste

To garnish

Shredded cabbage or lettuce

To serve

Red Salsa (page 234)

METHOD

Process the mayonnaise, cheese and sour cream in a blender until smooth. Fold in the remaining ingredients and pour into a shallow ovenproof dish. Bake in a hot oven until just heated. Warm the tortillas just before serving. Fill each tortilla with the hot corn mixture. Garnish with shredded cabbage or lettuce and fold over. Serve at once with salsa.

Hot Mexican Spinach Dip

INGREDIENTS **Serves 6-8**

½ cup Red Salsa (page 234)
2-3 black olives, chopped
6-8 fresh spinach leaves, washed and chopped
½ cup grated Monterey Jack or Cheddar cheese
¼ cup softened cream cheese
¼ cup cream
1 tbsp red wine vinegar
Salt and pepper to taste

To serve
Tortilla or taco chips

METHOD

Preheat the oven to 200°C/400°F/Gas Mark 6. In a medium-sized baking dish, mix together the salsa, olives, chopped spinach, grated cheese, cream cheese, cream, vinegar, salt and pepper. Bake for twelve to fifteen minutes or until bubbly. Serve hot with tortilla or taco chips.

Hot Mexican Spring Onion Dip

INGREDIENTS **Serves 12**

½ cup	Red Salsa (page 234)
1 bunch (6-8)	spring onions, finely chopped
½ cup	grated Monterey Jack cheese
¼ cup	cream cheese
¼ cup	thick cream
2-3 tbsp	finely chopped black olives
1 tsp	red wine vinegar
1 tsp	taco seasoning

Salt and pepper to taste

To serve
Taco chips

METHOD

Preheat the oven to 200°C/400°F/Gas Mark 6. In a medium-sized baking dish, mix all the ingredients and bake for 12-15 minutes or until bubbly. Serve with taco chips.

Indian-style Fondue
(Pav-Bhaji Fondue)

INGREDIENTS **Serves 4**

For the bhaji

1 tbsp	oil
1 medium	onion, finely chopped
1 tbsp	red chilli-garlic paste
1 tbsp	pav-bhaji masala
1 tsp	salt
2-3 medium	tomatoes, grated
1 cup	mixed vegetables (French beans, carrots, peas), finely chopped and boiled
2 tbsp	butter
½ cup	grated Cheddar cheese

Juice of 1 lemon

To garnish

Finely chopped coriander

To serve

Pav-bhaji bread, cut into cubes and toasted

METHOD

Heat oil in a frying pan; add the onion and chilli-garlic paste. Fry for 1 minute. Add pav-bhaji masala and salt along with a little water. Cook until well roasted and the oil separates from the spices. Add tomatoes and the boiled vegetables and mix well. Crush the vegetables with a potato masher; bring to a boil and remove from heat. Stir in the butter, lemon juice and cheese. When ready to serve, heat the mixture gently and pour into a fondue dish. Garnish with coriander and serve with the toasted bread.

Jacket Potato Chips with Jalapeño Sauce

INGREDIENTS **Serves 4**

6-8 small	potatoes, washed and soaked in water
¼ cup	olive oil
½ tsp	salt
½ tsp	pepper
½ tsp	chilli flakes

For the jalapeño sauce

2 tsp	butter
2 tsp	oil
2 tsp	chopped ginger
2 tsp	garlic, chopped
4 tbsp	finely chopped jalapeño chillies
2 tbsp	vinegar
2 tbsp	sugar
¼ cup	Sour Cream (page 234)

Salt to taste

METHOD

Cut the potatoes in one-fourth-inch thick slices. Heat the oil in a shallow pan and fry the potatoes in batches until crisp. Sprinkle each batch with salt, pepper and chilli flakes. Keep warm.

For the jalapeño sauce

Heat the butter and oil together in a small pan. Fry ginger, garlic and jalapeño chillies for 1 minute. Add a quarter cup of water, the vinegar, sugar and salt. Bring to a boil. Remove from heat and cool. Blend the mixture to a smooth purée and stir in the sour cream. Serve with the fried potatoes.

Note: You can store the sauce in the refrigerator before adding the sour cream.

Jalapeños Rellenos

INGREDIENTS **Serves 6**

12	fresh jalapeño chillies
½ cup	cream cheese
½ cup	Monterey Jack or Cheddar cheese
2	spring onion stems, finely chopped
¼ cup	plain flour
Salt to taste	
Oil for deep-frying	

METHOD

Wash and rinse the chillies. Slit the chillies on one side and remove the seeds and pith. Mix both the cheeses and spring onion and stuff the chillies with the mixture. Slightly overlap the edges to hold the filling inside. Mix the flour with a little water and a quarter teaspoon salt to make a thin paste. Roll each chilli in the flour paste to coat all over; gently shaking off the excess coating. Heat the oil over medium heat and fry the chillies, a few at a time, till golden brown. Drain on kitchen paper and serve immediately.

Note: For a crunchier coating, roll each flour-coated jalapeño chilli in breadcrumbs before frying.

Jalapeño Cheese Spread

INGREDIENTS **Makes 1 cup**

1¼ cups	grated Cheddar cheese
4-5	pimento stuffed olives
3	jalapeño chillies, finely chopped (approx. 2 tbsp)
1 tsp	vinegar
¼ cup	blanched and chopped red pepper
2-3 tbsp	Mayonnaise (page 230)
2 tbsp	finely chopped dill or herb of your choice

To serve

Melba toast or crackers

METHOD

Combine all the ingredients; mix well. Cover and refrigerate until chilled. Just before serving, spoon or spread on Melba toast or crackers and serve.

Kababs Stuffed with Greens
(Hara Bhara Kabab)

INGREDIENTS

Makes 12 kababs

2 cups	chopped spinach leaves
3-4 medium	potatoes, boiled, peeled and mashed
¾ cup	shelled green peas, boiled and crushed
1 tbsp	finely chopped coriander
1 tsp	chaat masala
1 tbsp	green chilli-ginger-garlic paste
2 tbsp	cornflour

A pinch of soda bicarbonate
Salt to taste
Oil for frying

To Serve

Green Chutney (page 236) mixed with a little yogurt

METHOD

Wash the spinach leaves and cook in 2 cups of boiling water with a pinch of soda bicarbonate for about 5 minutes. Drain completely and plunge into a bowl of ice cold water. Combine spinach, mashed potatoes, peas, coriander, chaat masala, chilli-ginger-garlic paste, salt and cornflour. Place the mixture in a refrigerator for 30 minutes. Remove and divide the mixture into 12 equal portions. Apply a little oil on your palms and shape each portion into 2-inch round flat kababs. Heat oil in a frying pan and either deep-fry or shallow fry them, 1-2 kababs at a time. Drain on kitchen paper.. Serve hot with green chutney.

Kung Pao Cottage Cheese
(Kung Pao Paneer)

INGREDIENTS **Serves 4**

300 gms	cottage cheese, cut into ½-inch cubes

For the marinade

1 tbsp	soy sauce
1 tbsp	chilli-garlic sauce
2 tbsp	tomato purée
2 tsp	cornflour
1 tsp	oil

¼ tsp salt

¼ tsp pepper

For stir-frying

4 tbsp	oil
7-8	dried red chillies
2 tbsp	ginger-garlic paste
1 tbsp	red chilli paste
2 tsp	soy sauce
1½ tbsp	sugar or plum sauce
½ tsp	chilli flakes
1½ tbsp	vinegar
1/3 cup	Vegetable Stock (page 166)
1 tbsp	cornflour

Salt to taste

To garnish

2 spring onion stems, cut into 3-inch pieces

METHOD

Mix the cottage cheese with all the ingredients for the marinade. Cover and set aside for 1 hour. Heat 2 tablespoons of oil in a heavy frying pan and fry the cottage cheese for 8-10 minutes. Drain and set aside. In the same pan, heat the remaining oil, add the chillies, ginger-garlic and chilli pastes and fry for 3-4 minutes. Add cottage cheese, soy sauce, sugar or plum sauce, salt, chilli flakes and vinegar. Add vegetable stock mixed with the cornflour. Stir to mix. Simmer and cook till the liquid is absorbed. Remove from heat and transfer to a serving plate. Garnish with spring onions and serve hot.

Layered Sandwiches

INGREDIENTS **Serves 6-8**

1 large — loaf unsliced sandwich bread
½ cup — butter, softened
Salt, pepper and mustard

For the cottage cheese spread

1 cup — crumbled cottage cheese
¼ cup — Sour Cream (page 234)
¼ cup — chopped red pepper
1 tbsp — chopped basil
1 tbsp — chopped green chillies
Salt and pepper to taste

For the olive and nut spread

½ cup — cream cheese spread
¼ cup — toasted and chopped walnuts
¼ cup — chopped olives
2 tbsp — milk

For the carrot, cucumber and cheese filling

½ cup — grated carrot
½ cup — grated cucumber
½ cup — grated processed cheese
1 tbsp — butter
1 tbsp — thick cream
Salt and pepper to taste

To garnish

Grated cabbage and carrot

METHOD

Slice the bread horizontally into 4 slices. Beat butter with salt, pepper and mustard. Spread the mixture evenly on the bread slices.

For the spreads

Mix all the ingredients for each spread or filling separately in 3 bowls.
Place 1 slice of buttered bread on a board and spread cottage cheese mixture evenly. Cover with another slice of bread and spread with olive and nut spread. Cover with the third slice and spread with the carrot, cucumber and cheese filling. Cover the top with the last slice of bread and press down lightly to seal. Cover with cling wrap and place in a refrigerator for half an hour. Remove and slice vertically into half-inch thick slices and arrange on a serving tray, garnished with grated carrots and cabbage.

Lemon Grass Spicy Vegetables

INGREDIENTS — Serves 4

For the vegetables

2 tbsp	oil
2 thick	lemon grass stalks
10-12	green beans, cut into 2-inch pieces
6-8	asparagus spears, cut into 2-inch pieces
250 gms	broccoli, separated into florets
4-6	baby corn cobs, cut diagonally into 1-inch pieces
1 medium	carrot, cut into thin matchsticks
¾ cup	bean curd, fried in a little oil
3 tbsp	Vegetable Stock (page 166)
2 tbsp	soy sauce
½ tsp	sugar

For the spice mixture

3	dried red chillies
1 tsp	chopped galangal
2 small	shallots, coarsely chopped
1 tbsp	finely chopped lemon grass
2-3 cloves	garlic, chopped
1 tbsp	grated fresh coconut

METHOD

In a mortar, pound together all the ingredients for the spice mixture and set aside. Heat oil in a frying pan and fry the paste and the lemon grass. Add all the vegetables and stir-fry for a few minutes. Add the stock, soy sauce and sugar. Stir well and transfer to a serving dish.

Lentil Crescents with Vegetable Yogurt Relish (Gujiya with Kosambari)

INGREDIENTS

Makes 12 crescents

For the covering

1 cup	plain flour
¼ cup	wholewheat flour
¼ cup	semolina
2 tbsp	hot ghee

A pinch of salt
Oil for deep-frying

For the filling

1 tbsp	oil
1 tsp	cumin seeds
4	green chillies, finely chopped
2 tbsp	finely chopped garlic
1 inch	ginger, finely grated
1 cup	green gram, soaked, cooked and ground to a paste
1 cup	grated cottage cheese
2 tsp	chaat masala
1 tsp	toasted sesame seeds
2 tsp	plain flour
2 tbsp	coriander

Salt to taste

To serve

Green Chutney (page 236), sliced onions and Kosambari (recipe follows)

METHOD

For the covering

Mix all the flours and salt. Make a well in the centre; pour hot ghee into it, cover and set aside for 10 minutes. Mix all the ingredients to make a soft dough, cover and allow to rest for half an hour.

For the filling

Heat oil in a frying pan; sauté cumin seeds, green chillies, garlic and ginger. Add green gram paste and cottage cheese and cook for 3-4 minutes. Add chaat masala, sesame seeds, flour, salt and coriander leaves. Continue cooking till the mixture is dry. Remove from heat and set aside to cool.

Divide the dough in 2 parts and roll each one out very thin. Cut out 3-inch rounds and fill each one with 1-2 tablespoons of filling. Fold over to shape like a half moon. Crimp the edges and seal. Deep-fry in hot oil and serve with green chutney and kosambari.

Kosambari

Makes 2½ cups

INGREDIENTS

1 tsp	oil
2	green chillies, slit
3-4	curry leaves
2 cups	thick yogurt
1 medium	carrot, grated
1 medium	cucumber, grated
1 medium	tomato, chopped
2 tbsp	crushed peanuts
2 tsp	sugar
½ tsp	cumin powder
½ tsp	chopped mint
1 tbsp	finely chopped coriander
Salt to taste	

METHOD

Heat oil in a small pan; add green chillies and curry leaves and sauté for 1 minute. Add to the yogurt. Add all the remaining ingredients and chill for 2-3 hours. Serve with snacks or parathas.

Lentil Waffles

INGREDIENTS **Makes 6-8 waffles**

1/3 cup	skinless split black gram
1/3 cup	split Bengal gram
1/3 cup	split lentils
1	tomato, finely chopped
1	onion, finely chopped
3-4	green chillies, finely chopped
¼ cup	finely chopped coriander
¼ tsp	turmeric
1 tbsp	oil + for greasing

A pinch of asafoetida
Salt to taste

To serve
Coconut Chutney (page 236)

METHOD

Soak all the lentils together for 3-4 hours and grind them with some water to make a coarse batter of dropping consistency. Mix all the other ingredients with the batter and set aside for 1 hour. Heat a waffle iron and brush it with a little oil. When the iron is very hot, pour enough mixture to cover all the corners of the iron and lightly close the lid. Cook till the waffles are golden brown. Serve hot with coconut chutney.

Note: If you don't have a waffle iron, make small pancakes on a non-stick frying pan.

Marinated Cottage Cheese with Crispy Noodles

INGREDIENTS **Serves 6**

500 gms	cottage cheese, cut into 1½-inch pieces
2 tsp	oil
1 medium	red pepper, cut into strips
100 gms	snow peas, asparagus or broccoli
8-10	shiitake mushrooms, soaked and sliced
100 gms	thin rice noodles, fried crisp

For the marinade

2 tbsp	tomato-chilli sauce
¼ cup	finely chopped lemon grass
¼ cup	finely chopped coriander
3 small	fresh red chillies, finely chopped
4 cloves	garlic, chopped
1 large	onion, grated

Salt to taste

To serve

Chilli sauce

METHOD

Combine all the ingredients for the marinade in a bowl; marinate cottage cheese in the mixture for 20 minutes. Heat oil in a wok, add red pepper, snow peas (or any other vegetables you are using) and mushrooms. Sauté for 2-3 minutes. Add marinated cottage cheese and stir-fry till heated through. Serve the cheese on a bed of fried rice noodles with chilli sauce on the side.

Mexican Corn Dip

INGREDIENTS

Serves 4-6

300 gms	tinned yellow corn kernels, drained
½ cup	grated Cheddar cheese
½ cup	Sour Cream (page 234), flavoured with 1 tsp each of garlic and chives
2	spring onion stems, finely chopped
3 tbsp	diced jalapeño chillies
¼ cup	diced blanched tomatoes
1 tsp	taco seasoning
¼ cup	Mayonnaise (page 230)

To serve

Taco chips, crackers or raw vegetables (crudités)

METHOD

Place the drained corn kernels in a bowl and crush them slightly. Beat the cheese and sour cream together. Add the rest of the ingredients and mix well. Cover and chill for one hour. Serve with chips, crackers or raw vegetables.

Mexican Corn Dip

Mini Coriander Cakes (Kothimbir Vadi)

Medley of Baby Vegetables

Oriental Vegetables with Peanut Sauce

INGREDIENTS **Serves 4-6**

2 tbsp	sesame oil
500 gms	vegetables (baby corn, snow peas, broccoli, water chestnuts, peppers) cut into 2-inch pieces

Salt to taste

For the peanut sauce

1 tbsp	sesame oil
1 tbsp	crushed garlic
1 tbsp	crushed ginger
1 tbsp	red chilli paste
3 tbsp	coarsely ground peanuts
3-4	kaffir lime leaves, thinly sliced
1 tbsp	sesame oil
1 tbsp	vinegar
½ cup	coconut milk mixed with 1 tsp cornflour
1 tsp	raw sugar
1 tsp	soy sauce

Salt to taste

To garnish

Sprigs of coriander

METHOD

For the peanut sauce

Heat oil in a small pan; add garlic, ginger and chilli paste. Fry until fragrant. Add the remaining ingredients and bring to a boil. Remove from heat and set aside.

For the vegetables

In a wok, heat oil over high heat and stir-fry the vegetables for 3 to 4 minutes. Add salt. When the vegetables are tender and crisp, pour the peanut sauce over. Toss gently to mix. Transfer to a serving dish, garnish with coriander sprigs and serve hot.

Oriental Vegetables with Peanut Sauce

Mixed Pepper Tartlets

Peppered Cheese Ball

Medley of Baby Vegetables

INGREDIENTS **Serves 4-6**

200 gms	baby corn
200 gms	baby carrots
200 gms	baby potatoes, parboiled
200 gms	snow peas
200 gms	broccoli florets
200 gms	Brussels sprouts
2 tbsp	butter
1 clove	garlic, crushed with a little salt
2 tbsp	Vegetable Stock (page 166)
2 tbsp	olive oil
2 tbsp	wine vinegar
1 tsp	sugar
1 tsp	salt
1 tsp	chilli flakes

A handful of fresh herbs (tarragon, basil, coriander or chives)

To garnish

Slivered and toasted almonds

To serve

Crusty bread

METHOD

Clean the vegetables. Cut the baby corn, carrots, snow peas and potatoes in half if desired. Melt the butter in a wok; sauté garlic for 1 minute. Add all the vegetables and the stock and cook over medium heat. In a small saucepan, heat olive oil, vinegar, sugar, salt and chilli flakes. Remove from heat and stir in the herbs. When the vegetables are cooked, but still slightly crunchy, stir in the herb mixture. Transfer to a warmed dish and garnish with slivered and toasted almonds. Serve with toothpicks or with crusty bread as a side dish.

Mexican Tortilla Appetisers

INGREDIENTS **Serves 12**

6	6-inch flour tortillas
2 cups	Refried Beans (page 235)
1 tbsp	taco sauce
½ cup	chopped red pepper
½ cup	chopped green pepper
½ cup	finely chopped spring onion
¼ tsp	chilli flakes
2 cups	mixed grated cheese (Monterey Jack, Cheddar, mozzarella)
To serve	
½ cup	Red Salsa (page 234)

METHOD

Preheat the oven to 200°C/400°F/Gas Mark 6. Place the tortillas on a baking sheet and bake for 3 to 4 minutes until crisp. Spread refried beans evenly on tortillas. Spread taco sauce over the beans. Top with peppers, spring onion and chilli flakes. Sprinkle with cheese. Bake for 7-8 minutes or until cheese melts. Cut into wedges and serve with the salsa.

Millet Pancakes
(Bajri Uttapam)

INGREDIENTS **Makes 4-5 pancakes**

¼ cup	whole millet grains, soaked
1 cup	millet flour
½ cup	yogurt
2 tbsp	chilli-ginger-garlic paste
1 medium	onion, diced
1 medium	tomato, diced
Oil	for greasing + for frying

Salt to taste

8-10 five-inch square pieces of banana leaf

To serve

Green Chutney (page 236) and fried green chillies

METHOD

Cook the millet grains in a pressure cooker till the pressure is released once (1 whistle). Mix millet flour and yogurt in a bowl to make a smooth batter. Cover and set aside for 1-2 hours. Just before making the uttapam, add the chilli-ginger-garlic paste, diced onion and tomato and salt to taste. If you find the batter too thick, add a little water. Heat a flat griddle, and brush it with a little oil. Brush the banana leaves with oil. Place 1 leaf on the griddle and spread 2-3 tablespoons of the prepared batter. Smoothen the surface. Sprinkle with cooked millet grains and cover with another leaf. Cover and cook over medium heat, turning over to cook the other side. Serve hot with green chutney and chillies.

Mini Coriander Cakes
(Kothimbir Vadi)

INGREDIENTS **Makes 25-30 pieces**

1 cup	chickpea flour
¼ cup	cashew nuts, broken into small pieces
3 tbsp	finely chopped coriander
1 tbsp	oil + for deep-frying
½ tsp	chilli powder
½ tsp	garam masala
Salt to taste	

To serve
Green Chutney (page 236)

METHOD

Make a thick batter of all the ingredients with 1 cup of water except the oil. Transfer the mixture to a thick-bottomed saucepan and cook over low heat, stirring continuously, until the mixture is thick and coats the back of the spoon. Pour the batter immediately into a 6-inch x 8-inch shallow, flat greased tin. Leave to cool for an hour. Cut into small cubes and deep-fry till golden brown. Serve with green chutney.

Mini Steamed Spinach and Tomato Cakes
(Palak-Tamatar Idlis)

INGREDIENTS — Serves 6-8

2 cups	idli batter
¼ cup	tomato purée
½ tsp	chilli powder
¼ cup	spinach purée
1 tsp	chopped green chillies

Salt to taste
Some oil to grease the mould

For the tempering

2 tbsp	clarified butter
½ tsp	mustard seeds
½ tsp	cumin seeds
½ tsp	white split gram

A pinch of asafoetida
A few curry leaves

To garnish
Grated fresh coconut and chopped coriander

To serve
Coconut Chutney (page 236)

METHOD

For the idlis
Divide the batter equally into two bowls. Add tomato purée, salt and chilli powder to one bowl of batter, and spinach, salt and green chillies to the other bowl. Lightly grease the cocktail idli moulds and pour 1 teaspoon of the batter in each mould. Steam the idlis for about 10-12 minutes. Remove, cool slightly and scoop them out of the moulds. Cover and set aside. Repeat for the remaining batter.

For the tempering
Heat clarified butter in a small pan and add mustard and cumin seeds. When they begin to crackle, add the split gram and asafoetida. When the gram turns golden brown, add the curry leaves and stir. Sprinkle the sizzling spices on the steamed idlis. Garnish with coriander and coconut and serve hot with coconut chutney.

Mini Tortilla Cups
(Antojitos Minis)

INGREDIENTS **Serves 6**

12 small	tortillas
2 tbsp	butter
½ cup	grated Cheddar cheese
½ cup	grated Monterey Jack cheese
½ cup	finely chopped red pepper
½ cup	boiled corn kernels
1/3 cup	finely chopped spring onions
1/3 cup	boiled black beans
2 tbsp	Red Salsa (page 234)
1 tbsp	taco seasoning
Oil for greasing	

METHOD

Lightly grease cupcake moulds with a little oil. Brush each tortilla with butter. Preheat the oven to 220°C/425°F/Gas Mark 7. Insert the tortilla into the cups and lightly press down to get the shape of the cup. Bake for 10-15 minutes till light brown. Remove from the moulds and set aside to cool. Mix both cheeses together and place some of the mixture at the bottom of each tortilla cup. Top with red pepper, corn, spring onion, black beans, salsa and taco seasoning. Place the cups on a baking sheet and bake for 5 minutes or till the cheese browns slightly. Remove and serve hot.

Minted Pea and Yogurt Dip

INGREDIENTS **Makes 1½ cups**

1 cup thick yogurt
2 tbsp chopped fresh mint
1/3 cup boiled green peas
2-3 tbsp Parmesan cheese
Salt and pepper to taste
Juice of ½ a lemon

To serve
Vegetable crudités such as carrot, asparagus, radish, baby corn.

METHOD

Process yogurt and mint in a blender for 1 minute. Add the peas and Parmesan cheese and blend again. Transfer to a bowl and add salt, pepper and lemon juice. Serve cold or at room temperature with chilled crudités.

Mixed Pepper Tartlets

INGREDIENTS — **Makes 12-14 tartlets**

12-14 small	tart cases
2 tbsp	butter
2 medium	onions, chopped
2 medium	red and yellow peppers, chopped
2 tbsp	plain flour
1 cup	milk
1 packet	asparagus or vegetable soup powder
½ cup	thick cream
¾ cup	grated Cheddar cheese
2 tbsp	chopped pine nuts
¼ cup	finely chopped spring onion

Salt and pepper to taste

METHOD

Preheat the oven to 180°C/350°F/Gas Mark 4. Melt 1 tablespoon butter in a frying pan; sauté onion and peppers until soft. Set aside. In a saucepan, melt remaining butter, add the flour and cook until the mixture turns slightly pale in colour. Remove from heat and add milk, salt, pepper and soup mix. Return the mixture to the heat and bring it to a boil. Gently stir in the cream and cheese and cook, stirring continuously until the cheese melts. Add pine nuts and spring onion and mix well. Spoon the onion-pepper mixture into the tart cases. Pour 1-2 tablespoons of the cheese-cream sauce over the filling and bake in the preheated oven for 5-7 minutes. Serve immediately.

Mixed Vegetable Kababs
(Sabji ke Kabab)

INGREDIENTS **Serves 8-10**

500 gms	potatoes, boiled and mashed
1 cup	finely chopped boiled mixed vegetables (such as carrot, potato, green peas, cauliflower)
2 tsp	ginger-garlic paste
1 tsp	chilli powder
¼ tsp	turmeric powder
¾ cup	yogurt, beaten
2 tbsp	cashew nuts or almonds, ground
125 gms	chickpea flour, roasted

Juice of 2 lemons
Salt to taste
Oil for frying

To garnish
2 thinly sliced onions, fried; 4-5 lemon slices and a few mint

To serve
Mint Chutney (page 236)

METHOD

Mix together mashed potatoes, vegetables, ginger-garlic paste, chilli powder, turmeric powder and salt. Use a potato masher to mix them well. Add yogurt, nuts, chickpea flour and lemon juice and mix well. For each kabab, take about 1 tablespoon of mixture on your palm and roll it into a 2½-inch long oblong shape. When ready to serve, deep-fry in hot oil until golden. You can also shallow-fry them in a frying pan or barbecue them on skewers. Garnish with sliced onions, lemon slices and mint leaves and serve with mint chutney.

Muffaletta Pizza

INGREDIENTS **Serves 4-6**

4	8-inch thin pizza bases
1 tbsp	olive oil
1 tsp	garlic salt
1 cup	grated mozarella cheese
1 tsp	chilli flakes
For the olive salad	
8	black olives, sliced
3-4	sun-dried tomatoes, soaked and chopped
2 tbsp	chopped celery
2 tbsp	chopped red pepper
2 tbsp	chopped onion
2 cloves	garlic, chopped
1 tbsp	chopped parsley
1 tbsp	chopped basil
½ tsp	dried oregano
½ tsp	salt
½ tsp	pepper
2 tbsp	olive oil

METHOD

For the olive salad, mix together all the ingredients in a medium bowl, cover and chill in the refrigerator until ready to use.

Preheat the oven to 200°C/400°F/Gas Mark 6. Sprinkle pizza bases with olive oil and garlic salt. Place the pizzas directly on the oven rack and bake for 5 minutes. Do not allow the pizzas to brown too much. Remove from heat and allow to cool slightly. Remove olive salad from the refrigerator and add the cheese and chilli flakes. Toss gently to mix. Spread evenly on the 4 pizza bases. Place the pizzas, one at a time, under a hot grill for 5 minutes or until the cheese melts. Cut into wedges and serve.

Nacho Cheese Fondue

INGREDIENTS **Serves 6**

1 tsp	butter
1 clove	garlic, crushed
½ cup	white wine
½ cup	Red Salsa (page 234)
2 tbsp	finely chopped jalapeño chillies
1 tbsp	taco seasoning
250 gms	nacho cheese, cut into cubes
To garnish	
½ tsp	chilli flakes
1 tbsp	finely chopped spring onion
To serve	
2 cups	taco chips

METHOD

Heat a fondue pot; add butter and rub the inside of the fondue pot with the garlic clove. Add wine. When it starts to boil, add salsa, jalapeño chillies, taco seasoning and the cheese. Stir constantly to blend. When all the cheese has melted and the mixture is smooth, remove from heat. Garnish with chilli flakes and spring onion. Place the fondue pot over a burner and serve with taco chips.

Note: For a non-alcoholic fondue, replace white wine with vegetable stock (page166).

Nacho Cheese Party Melt

INGREDIENTS **Serves 4-6**

1½ tsp	taco seasoning
¼ cup	melted butter
4 cups	popcorn
1 cup	tortilla chips
1 cup	potato cubes
1 cup	bread stick pieces
1 cup	grated Cheddar or Monterey Jack cheese

METHOD

Preheat the oven to 150°C/300°F/Gas Mark 2. Stir taco seasoning mix into the melted butter. Toss the popcorn, tortilla chips, potato cubes and bread sticks into the butter mixture. Spread the mixture on a baking sheet lined with foil. Sprinkle with cheese and bake for 5-7 minutes or till the cheese melts. Serve immediately.

Nine-layer Mediterranean Dip

INGREDIENTS **Serves 12-14**

200 gms	cream cheese
100 gms	feta cheese, crumbled
1 tbsp	Italian seasoning
1 cup	grated Parmesan cheese
2 medium	red peppers, roasted, peeled and coarsely chopped
½ cup	sautéed eggplant
1	spring onion stem, finely chopped
½ cup	chopped black olives
¼ cup	toasted and chopped pine nuts

To garnish

Freshly chopped mixed herbs

To serve

Pita chips, Melba toasts or crackers

METHOD

Combine cream cheese, feta cheese and Italian seasoning in a food processor or blender, or with a hand beater in a bowl. Line a 4-cup capacity bowl with cling wrap or foil, allowing 8 inches of wrap to extend over the sides of the bowl. Layer ingredients in the following order: half the Parmesan cheese, half the roasted peppers and eggplant, half the cream cheese mixture, spring onion, olives, pine nuts, remaining peppers and eggplant, remaining cream cheese mixture and remaining Parmesan cheese. Fold the wrap over the top and refrigerate until firm and ready to serve. This may be made a day ahead.

To serve, remove from refrigerator and undo the plastic wrap. Place serving plate face down on top of the bowl. Turn the bowl over and gently lift it. Carefully peel off cling wrap. Garnish with fresh herbs and serve with pita chips, Melba toasts or crackers.

Olive and Pepper Wheels

INGREDIENTS

Serves 6-8

For the tomato paste

¼ cup	sun-dried tomatoes, roughly chopped
¼ cup	pine nuts
3 tbsp	grated Parmesan cheese
1 tbsp	olive oil

Salt and pepper to taste

For the peppers

2	red peppers, roasted and peeled
2	yellow peppers, roasted and peeled
1/3 cup	olive oil
1 tsp	balsamic vinegar
2 cloves	garlic, crushed
½ tbsp	dried thyme

Salt and pepper to taste

To assemble the pizzas

4 thin	6-inch pizza bases
¼ cup	sliced olives
1 tbsp	fresh thyme
6	cheese slices

METHOD

Preheat the oven to 180°C/350°F/Gas Mark 4.

For the tomato paste

Process all the ingredients in a food processor or blender.

For the peppers

Slice the peppers into long strips and place them in a bowl. Add olive oil, balsamic vinegar, garlic, thyme, salt and pepper. Marinate at room temperature for 1 hour.

To assemble the pizzas

Spread tomato paste evenly over all 4 pizza bases. Arrange marinated pepper slices all round the pizzas and place sliced olives in the centre. Sprinkle with fresh thyme and cover with cheese slices. Bake for 10 minutes. Remove from the oven, cut into wedges and serve.

Olive-Cheese Bites

INGREDIENTS **Makes 24 appetisers**

24 medium	pimento-stuffed olives
¼ cup	butter
¼ cup	grated Cheddar cheese
1/3 + ¼ cup	sifted plain flour
A dash of salt	

METHOD

Pat the olives dry with a thick paper towel. Cut butter and cheese into the flour. Add salt and mix into a dough. Shape into small balls around the olives. Chill for several hours or overnight in the refrigerator. Bake on a greased baking sheet in a hot oven at 200°C/400°F/Gas Mark 6 for 15 minutes. Serve warm.

Oriental Croquettes in Noodle Wraps

INGREDIENTS **Serves 6**

1 tbsp sesame oil
1 tbsp garlic paste
1 tbsp ginger paste
1 tbsp red chilli paste
2 spring onion stems, finely chopped
1 cup finely chopped vegetables (cabbage, carrot, beans)
250 gms potatoes, boiled and mashed
1 tsp soy sauce
1 tbsp finely chopped coriander
1 tbsp cornflour
1½ cups boiled hakka noodles
Juice of half a lemon
Salt to taste
A pinch of soda bicarbonate
Oil for deep-frying

To serve
Chilli-garlic sauce

METHOD

Heat oil in a frying pan; fry garlic, ginger and red chilli paste for 1 minute. Add spring onions and the vegetables and cook until soft. Remove from heat and cool. Add to the mashed potatoes along with soy sauce, coriander leaves, cornflour, lemon juice, salt and soda bicarbonate. Mix well. Grease your palms with a little oil, take 2 tablespoons of mixture and shape into a cylindrical croquette. Take a handful of noodles and place on a board and wrap around each croquette. Fry croquettes in hot oil till noodles turn golden. Serve hot with chilli-garlic sauce.

Pan-fried Dumplings

INGREDIENTS **Serves 6**

250 gms	bean curd, crumbled
½ tsp	sesame seeds
½ tsp	cornflour
½ tsp	salt
1 tsp	sesame oil
1 tsp	chopped green chillies
1 tsp	chopped garlic
2 tbsp	finely chopped spring onions
12-15	wonton wrappers
4 tbsp	sunflower oil

To serve

Korean Soy Sauce (recipe follows)

METHOD

In a small bowl, mix together bean curd, sesame seeds, cornflour, salt, sesame oil, chillies, garlic and spring onions. Place 1 tablespoon of mixture in the centre of each wonton wrapper and fold it across to make a triangle; twist both the tips to make a hat shaped dumpling. Bring a large pan of water to a boil and drop in 3 to 4 dumplings at a time. Remove from water and cool for 3 minutes. Stir-fry cooked wontons in sunflower oil till golden. Remove and drain. Serve hot with Korean Soy Sauce.

Korean Soy Sauce **Makes 1/3 cup**

In a serving bowl, mix together 3 tbsp soy sauce, 1 tbsp chopped spring onions and 1 tsp each of sesame seeds, oil, chopped red chilli, crushed garlic, sugar and vinegar.

Papad Paneer Snack

INGREDIENTS **Serves 4**

250 gms	cottage cheese, cubed
2-3 tbsp	Szechwan sauce
½ tsp	dried mango powder
½ tsp	black salt
½ tsp	chilli powder
½ tsp	salt
½ cup	yogurt
2 large	moong or udad papads, roasted and crushed

Oil for deep-frying

To serve

Green Chutney (page 236) mixed with a little yogurt

METHOD

Slit the cottage cheese and fill a little Szechwan sauce inside each cube. Set aside. Mix all the dry spices with yogurt and soak stuffed cottage cheese in the mixture for about 5-10 minutes. Remove each piece of cottage cheese and roll it in roasted papad crumbs. Deep-fry in batches in hot oil until crisp. Drain on kitchen paper and serve hot with green chutney.

Parmesan and Pesto Toasts

INGREDIENTS **Makes 20-24**

1	long loaf French bread (baguette)
12-14	sun-dried tomatoes, thinly sliced
½ cup	grated Parmesan cheese
For the pesto	
1 cup	fresh basil
2 tbsp	freshly chopped chives
4 tbsp	toasted pine nuts
2-3 cloves	garlic
¼ cup	olive oil
½ tsp	salt
½ tsp	pepper

METHOD

Place the bread in the freezer for half an hour until firm. Cut into thick slices. Toast on a hot grill till golden brown on both sides.

For the pesto

Place all the ingredients in a small blender jar and blend until smooth.

Spread pesto evenly on the toasted slices. Top with sun-dried tomato slices and Parmesan cheese. Serve at room temperature or grill for 1 minute and serve.

Party Pita Wedges

INGREDIENTS **Makes 16 appetisers**

4 tbsp olive oil
2 large cloves garlic, finely chopped
¼ tsp dried oregano
¼ tsp salt
¼ tsp pepper
1 tbsp butter
2 6-inch pita breads
½ cup sun-dried tomatoes, soaked and sliced
1/3 cup sliced black olives
100 gms feta cheese
1 tbsp Harissa (page 47)
100 gms sliced cheese
Sea salt to taste

To garnish
Chopped parsley

METHOD

Preheat the oven to 190°C/375°F/Gas Mark 5. In a small bowl or pan, heat 3 tbsp olive oil, garlic, oregano, salt and pepper for 40 seconds in a microwave oven or 1 minute over heat. Remove and stir in butter. Cut both the pita breads into 4 pizza-shaped wedges. Slit each wedge again horizontally in half. Brush both sides of the pita with the warm olive oil mixture. Place wedges crust side down on a baking sheet. Mix together sun-dried tomatoes, olives, feta cheese, harrissa and 1 tablespoon olive oil in bowl. Divide equally among the wedges and spread evenly. Cover the wedges with sliced cheese. Drizzle with any remaining olive oil and sprinkle with sea salt. Bake for 15 minutes, or until cheese is bubbly. Serve hot, garnished with parsley.

Pattaya Baby Corn and Bean Curd

INGREDIENTS **Serves 4**

100 gms	baby corn, cut into 2-inch sticks
3-4 tbsp	vegetable oil
1 tbsp	sugar
1 tbsp	light soy sauce
100 gms	bean curd, cut into 2-inch sticks
2 tbsp	kaffir lime leaves, shredded

For the spice mixture

3-4	dried red chillies
3 cloves	garlic
1 tsp	grated galangal
½ tsp	coriander seeds
½ tsp	chopped coriander root
1 tbsp	thinly sliced shallots
2 tbsp	finely chopped lemon grass
½ tsp	grated lemon rind
1 tsp	salt

To garnish

Vertically sliced spring onions and sliced lime leaves

METHOD

Grind together all the ingredients for the spice mixture with a mortar and pestle until well ground. Blanch baby corn in boiling water for 3 minutes and drain. In a wok or a frying pan, heat oil. Fry the spice mixture until it is dry and fragrant; season with sugar and soy sauce. Add baby corn and bean curd and mix thoroughly with the spices. Sprinkle a little water if the mixture turns too dry or sticks to the pan. Cook for 5-7 minutes. Transfer to a serving plate and sprinkle sliced spring onions and lime leaves. Serve with toothpicks.

Pepper and Herb Fondue

INGREDIENTS **Serves 6**

2 cups	grated Emmental or Gruyère cheese
2 tbsp	cornflour
1 tbsp	butter
1 cup	finely chopped red and yellow peppers
1 tbsp	finely chopped garlic
2 tbsp	freshly chopped herbs of your choice
1½ cups	Vegetable Stock (page 166)
1 cup	milk

Salt and pepper to taste
Dash of balsamic vinegar

To serve
Cubes of toasted French bread (croutons) or boiled baby potatoes

METHOD

Toss the cheese in cornflour and set aside. Melt butter in a fondue dish; sauté peppers and garlic till peppers are cooked but not mushy. Stir in the herbs, stock and milk. Bring to a boil and then add the cheese mixture a little at a time, stirring in figure 8 movements after each addition. This way you make sure that it doesn't stick to the bottom of the dish. Season with salt, pepper and a dash of balsamic vinegar, and cook till thick. Serve hot with toasted bread cubes and baby potatoes.

Party Mix

INGREDIENTS **Makes approximately 1 kg**

2-3 tbsp	oil
½ cup	peanuts, skinned
½ cup	roasted Bengal gram
½ cup	split Bengal gram
1 tbsp	chaat masala
1 tbsp	chilli powder
1 tbsp	dried mango powder
1 tsp	black salt
1 tsp	cumin powder
1 tsp	sesame seeds
100 gms	fried small papads
100 gms	potato straws
100 gms	lotus seed puffs
100 gms	sago wafers
100 gms	beaten rice
100 gms	sliced fresh coconut
100 gms	popcorn

Salt and sugar to taste

METHOD

In a wide pan, heat oil and add peanuts, roasted and split Bengal gram. Fry for 2-3 minutes. Mix all the spices in a small bowl. Add the remaining ingredients to the pan along with the spices, salt and sugar. Remove from heat and set aside to cool. Store in an airtight container.

Party Mix
Garden Vegetable Pizza
Spinach and Feta Cheese Cigars

Pesto and Feta Cheese Bruschetta

INGREDIENTS **Makes 14 pieces**

¼ cup	Pesto Sauce (page 233)
12-14 small	Melba toasts
1 tbsp	olive oil
¼ tsp	chilli powder
1 tbsp	crushed garlic
4-5	fresh basil, finely chopped
¼ cup	crumbled feta cheese
2 medium	red tomatoes, finely chopped

Salt and pepper to taste

METHOD

Spread pesto sauce thinly on each toast. In a medium bowl, mix together olive oil, chilli powder, garlic, basil, salt and pepper. Add feta cheese and tomatoes. Toss gently to mix. Spoon the mixture onto the pesto-lined melba toasts and serve immediately.

Roasted Red Pepper and Walnut Spread

Pickled Cottage Cheese Kababs

Pesto and Feta Cheese Bruschetta

Pepper Cream Vegetables

INGREDIENTS **Serves 4**

2 tbsp	olive oil
500 gms	assorted vegetables (such as carrot, zucchini, eggplant, red capsicum, mushroom), sliced
250 gms	onions, thinly sliced
1 large clove	garlic, crushed
½ cup	Vegetable Stock (page 166)
½ cup	cream
3-4	fresh basil, chopped
2 tbsp	coarsely ground black pepper
Salt to taste	

METHOD

Apply 1 tablespoon of olive oil to the vegetables and cook them briefly on a grill for 3-4 minutes. Heat the remaining oil in a wok and fry onions and garlic for a few minutes. Add all the vegetables and stir-fry until tender and crisp. Mix together the stock, cream, basil, pepper and salt. Stir the mixture into the vegetables and cook, stirring continuously, until the sauce thickens slightly. Serve immediately with toothpicks.

Peppered Cheese Ball

INGREDIENTS **Makes one 5-inch ball**

2 cups	grated Cheddar or Monterey Jack cheese
1½ cups	cheese spread
½ cup	thick cream
1 tsp	chopped chives
1 tsp	parsley
1 tsp	Worcestershire sauce
2 cloves	garlic, crushed
2-3 tbsp	coarsely ground black, white and red pepper

Olive oil to grease the mould

To serve

Crackers and Melba toasts

METHOD

Beat together both the cheeses in a medium-sized bowl until creamy. Fold in the cream, herbs, Worcestershire sauce and garlic. Grease a 2-cup capacity mould with olive oil and dust generously with crushed pepper. Fill with the cheese mixture, spread evenly and cover with cling wrap. Refrigerate for 6 hours or overnight. Cut into thin slices and serve with crackers or Melba toasts.

Pickled Cottage Cheese Kababs
(Achaari Paneer Tikka)

INGREDIENTS

Serves 4

For the paneer tikka

250 gms	cottage cheese, cubed
2 tsp	cornflour
1 tbsp	oil
1 tbsp	sugar
2-3 tbsp	vinegar

For the marinade

1 tbsp	oil
1 tsp	mustard seeds
1 tsp	cumin seeds
1 tsp	fenugreek seeds
1 tsp	nigella seeds
1 tsp	aniseed
1 tbsp	ginger-garlic paste
1 medium	onion, grated
1 tbsp	vinegar
1 tsp	red chilli powder
1 tsp	garam masala
1 tsp	salt
1 cup	yogurt, beaten

To serve

Sliced onions and lemon wedges

METHOD

For the marinade

Heat oil in a small saucepan; add mustard, cumin, fenugreek, nigella seeds and aniseed. When they begin to crackle, add ginger-garlic paste and grated onion. Cook until soft. Add vinegar, chilli powder, garam masala and salt. Stir until well mixed. Add yogurt, mix well and remove from heat.

For the paneer tikka

Roll cottage cheese cubes in cornflour, soak them in the yogurt mixture and set aside for 2 hours. Thread the cottage cheese pieces onto skewers. Heat oil in a frying pan and place 2-3 skewers at a time in the pan. Cook the cottage cheese on both sides till slightly golden brown. Mix sugar and vinegar in a small bowl, sprinkle a little of this mixture on the cottage cheese and serve hot with sliced onions and lemon wedges.

Pink Yam Pancakes
(Kand na Pudla)

INGREDIENTS **Serves 4-6**

500 gms	grated pink yam
250 gms	potatoes, peeled and grated
2 tbsp	peanuts, coarsely powdered
4 tbsp	semolina
2-3	green chillies, chopped
1 inch	ginger, grated
2 tbsp	chopped coriander
2 tbsp	grated coconut
1-2 tbsp	yogurt

Salt to taste
Oil for frying

To serve
Green Chutney (page 236)

METHOD

In a large bowl, mix all the ingredients except oil. Whisk vigorously with a rounded spoon. When ready to serve, heat oil in a frying pan and drop 1-2 tablespoons of the mixture to form 3-inch round pancakes, 2-3 at a time. Cook on both sides and serve hot with green chutney.

Pink Yam Pie
(Kand no Handvo)

INGREDIENTS

Serves 6-8

1 kg	pink yam, boiled and mashed
4 medium	potatoes, boiled and mashed
1 tbsp	arrowroot powder
2-3 tbsp	thick yogurt
2-3 tbsp	oil
2 tbsp	green chilli-ginger paste
2 cups	shelled green peas, boiled and crushed
4 tbsp	freshly grated coconut
4 tbsp	chopped coriander

Salt to taste
Juice of 1 lemon
Sugar to taste

For the tempering

2 tbsp	oil
1 tsp	mustard seeds
1 tsp	sesame seeds
4-5	round red chillies

A few curry leaves

To garnish
Freshly grated coconut and chopped coriander

To serve
Coconut Sauce (recipe follows) or Green Chutney (page 236)

METHOD

For the tempering
Heat oil in a small pan; add mustard and sesame seeds and when they begin to crackle, add chillies and curry leaves.

Preheat the oven to 170^{0}C/325^{0}F/Gas Mark 3. Mix together mashed yam, potatoes, arrowroot and yogurt, season with salt and lemon juice to taste. In a frying pan, heat 2 tablespoons oil and fry green chilli-ginger paste briefly. Add green peas, sugar, salt and the remaining lemon juice. Remove from heat and leave to cool.

In an 8-inch x 10-inch baking dish, spread half the yam and potato mixture, layer the green pea mixture on top and spread evenly. Spread the remaining yam and potato mixture over the pea mixture. Smoothen the top with your palm. Drizzle the prepared tempering all over and bake in the preheated oven for 20-25 minutes. Leave to cool for 4-5 minutes and cut into 1-inch square pieces. Garnish with coriander and coconut. Serve hot with green chutney or coconut sauce.

Coconut Sauce
Heat 1 tsp oil; add a pinch of cumin seeds and 4-5 curry leaves. Add to 1 cup coconut milk. Add salt and sugar to taste. Sprinkle grated coconut and finely chopped coriander and serve warm or cold.

Pizza Snack

INGREDIENTS **Serves 6**

1 cup	grated mozzarella cheese
½ tsp	dried oregano
½ tsp	chilli flakes
½ tsp	garlic powder
¼ cup	finely chopped green or black olives
¼ cup	finely chopped capsicum
¼ cup	finely chopped onions, sautéed
1 tbsp	finely chopped basil
6-8	cream crackers

To garnish

Grilled tomato slices

METHOD

Preheat the oven to 150°C/300°C/Gas Mark 2. Mix all the ingredients except the crackers in a bowl. Spread 1-2 tablespoons of the mixture on each cracker. Arrange on a baking sheet and bake for 7-8 minutes, or until the cheese melts. Cut each cracker in half and serve hot, garnished with grilled tomato slices.

Potato and Sago Flatbreads
(Aloo aur Sabudana Thalipeeth)

INGREDIENTS — **Makes 15 appetisers**

150 gms	dried sago
1 cup	buttermilk
250 gms	thalipeeth flour
250 gms	potatoes, boiled and mashed
150 gms	roasted and powdered peanuts
1 tbsp	ginger-chilli paste
1 tbsp	chopped fresh coriander
¼ cup	yogurt
¼ cup	clarified butter
Salt to taste	

To serve

Coconut-Peanut Chutney (recipe follows)

METHOD

Soak the sago in buttermilk for 2 hours. Drain. Mix all the ingredients, except the clarified butter, and make a soft dough. Divide the dough into 12-15 balls. Roll out each ball into a 2-inch round and roast on a hot griddle with a little clarified butter. Turn over and cook the underside. Serve hot with coconut-peanut chutney.

Coconut-Peanut Chutney — **Makes ½ cup**

Roast together in 2 tbsp oil, 10 dried red chillies, 1 tbsp Bengal gram, 1 tbsp white gram, ¼ cup grated dried coconut, ¼ cup powdered peanuts and 1 tbsp sesame seeds. Cool and grind to a fine powder.

Potato Pancakes

INGREDIENTS **Makes 20 pancakes**

450 gms	potatoes, washed, peeled and grated
2 tbsp	milk
2 tbsp	plain flour
¼ cup	grated processed cheese
1 tsp	salt
1 tsp	pepper
1 tsp	Italian seasoning or mixed herbs
1 tbsp	olive oil
1 cup	grated carrot
1 cup	grated zucchini

To serve

Sour Cream (page 234), flavoured with basil and chives

METHOD

Preheat the oven to 220°C/425°F/Gas Mark 7. Wrap the grated potatoes in several layers of kitchen paper and squeeze to remove all the liquid. In a bowl, mix together milk, flour, cheese, salt, pepper and seasoning. Add the potato, carrot and zucchini and mix together. Grease 2 baking sheets. Place heaped tablespoons of the vegetable mixture onto the baking sheet and flatten to make pancakes. Bake the pancakes for 10-15 minutes or until the bottoms are browned. Turn over and bake for 5 minutes more. Serve hot with sour cream.

Potato Pizza Nests

INGREDIENTS **Serves 8-10**

1 cup	thick Marinara Sauce (page 232)
$^{1}/_{4}$ cup	finely chopped olives
$^{1}/_{4}$ cup	finely chopped pepper
$^{1}/_{2}$-1 tsp	chilli flakes
8-10	potato baskets
1 cup	grated mozzarella cheese

METHOD

Preheat the oven to 150°C/300°F/Gas Mark 2. Mix together the marinara sauce, chopped olives, pepper and chilli flakes in a bowl. Make sure the sauce is not watery; if necessary drain the liquid before mixing. Heat the potato baskets slightly in the oven to make them crisp. Spoon 2 tablespoons of marinara sauce mixture into the basket and top with 1 teaspoon of grated cheese to fit the size of the basket. Bake in the preheated oven for 5-7 minutes or until the cheese melts. Serve hot, sprinkled with additional chilli flakes.

Potato Wheels

INGREDIENTS **Serves 4**

2 medium	potatoes, washed and cut into ¼-inch slices
1 medium	zucchini, sliced and grilled
1 cup	Corn Salsa (recipe follows)
¼ cup	sliced jalapeño chillies
½ cup	grated Monterey Jack cheese

Oil for greasing
Butter or olive oil, to brush

To serve
Sour Cream (page 234)

METHOD

Preheat the oven to 180°C/350°F/Gas Mark 4. Arrange the potato slices on a greased baking sheet. Brush each slice with butter or olive oil and bake for 7-8 minutes. Remove from the oven and turn them over. Top each slice with grilled zucchini, 1 tablespoon of corn salsa, a slice of jalapeño and some grated cheese. Bake again until the cheese melts. Serve hot with sour cream and additional salsa.

Corn Salsa **Makes 1 cup**

In a bowl, mix together 2-3 chopped tomatoes, 1 small chopped onion, ½ cup crushed and boiled corn kernels, 1 tbsp chopped fresh coriander, 1 tbsp vinegar, 1 tbsp chopped jalapeño chillies, 1 tbsp red chilli paste, ½ tsp salt, ½ tsp taco seasoning and ½ tsp oregano.

Quick Pizza Sticks

Makes 24 pieces

INGREDIENTS

2	6-inch pizza bases
1 tbsp	melted butter
½ cup	grated mozzarella cheese
1 tbsp	grated Parmesan cheese
1 tsp	dried basil leaves
¼ tsp	garlic powder
¼ tsp	chilli flakes

To serve

Marinara Sauce (page 232)

METHOD

Preheat the oven to 220°C/425°F/Gas Mark 7. Lightly grease a large baking sheet. Brush pizza bases with melted butter. In a small bowl, combine the cheeses, basil, garlic powder and chilli flakes. Sprinkle evenly over the pizzas. With a pizza cutter or knife, mark the bases crossways into 1-inch wide strips and then in half along the centre. Do not cut right through. Bake for 10-12 minutes or till golden brown. To separate the sticks, re-cut along the marks. Serve immediately with warm marinara sauce.

Ranch-style Bean Dip

INGREDIENTS **Serves 8**

¼ cup	butter
1 small	onion chopped
1 clove	garlic, chopped
2	spring onion stems, finely chopped
1	jalapeño chilli, chopped
2 medium	tomatoes, blanched and chopped
1 tsp	dried oregano
1 tbsp	taco seasoning
2 cups	boiled and mashed kidney beans
1 cup	grated Monterey Jack cheese
½ cup	thick yogurt or Sour Cream (page 234)
Salt to taste	

To serve
Tortilla chips

METHOD

In a medium frying pan, melt butter. Add the onion, garlic, spring onion and jalapeño chilli and sauté until tender. Add the tomatoes, oregano, taco seasoning, mashed beans, salt and the cheese. Cook over low heat until the cheese melts. Just before removing from heat, stir in the yogurt or sour cream. Spoon into a small fondue pot and serve hot with tortilla chips.

Note: In place of 2 cups boiled and mashed kidney beans you can use tinned refried beans.

Red Pepper Hummus

INGREDIENTS **Serves 6**

200 gms chickpeas, soaked overnight and boiled
4-5 tbsp tahina paste
4-5 tbsp lemon juice
2 cloves garlic
2 medium red peppers, roasted and peeled
½ tsp dried basil
Salt and pepper to taste

To garnish
Olive oil, chilli flakes and fresh basil leaves

To serve
Crisp pita triangles

METHOD

Process all the ingredients together in a blender until smooth. Transfer to a serving bowl and make a design with a fork. Drizzle olive oil, sprinkle chilli flakes and decorate with basil leaves. Serve at room temperature with crisp pita bread.

Red Pepper Mousse

INGREDIENTS **Serves 4-6**

1 tbsp	unflavoured gelatine
¼ cup	Vegetable Stock (recipe follows)
1 tbsp	olive oil
1 tbsp	chopped garlic
500 gms	red peppers, roasted and peeled
1 tbsp	grenadine syrup
1 tbsp	lemon juice
2 tbsp	Mayonnaise (page 230)
½ cup	grated processed cheese
½ cup	fresh cream

Salt and pepper to taste

To garnish

A sprig of parsley and toasted pine nuts

To serve

Crisp bread or crackers

METHOD

Dissolve the gelatine in the vegetable stock. Heat oil in a frying pan and fry garlic and peppers for 2-3 minutes. Remove from heat and set aside to cool. Place sautéed peppers and garlic in a blender and add grenadine syrup, lemon juice, mayonnaise, grated cheese, salt and pepper. Blend until smooth. With the motor running, add the gelatine mixture in a thin stream. Transfer the mixture to a bowl. Beat the cream to form soft peaks and fold into the pepper mixture. Transfer to a serving bowl and refrigerate until set. Garnish with parsley and pine nuts. Serve with crisp bread or crackers.

Vegetable Stock **Makes 1 cup**

To make 1 cup vegetable stock, dissolve 1 vegetable stock cube in 1 cup of boiling water. Leave to cool and use as required.

Roasted Mixed Nuts

INGREDIENTS **Makes 2 cups**

100 gms	cashew nuts
100 gms	almonds
100 gms	peanuts
100 gms	lotus seed puffs
1-2 tbsp	clarified butter
1 tsp	salt
1 tsp	dried mango powder
1 tsp	coarsely ground black peppercorns

METHOD

Dry roast the nuts and lotus seed puffs and set aside. In a thick-bottomed pan, heat clarified butter and add the roasted nuts. Fry for 30 seconds. Add the salt and spices and fry again until the nuts are covered with the spices. Remove from heat and set aside to cool. Store in an airtight jar.

Roasted Red Pepper and Walnut Spread

INGREDIENTS **Makes $1\frac{1}{2}$ cups**

200 gms	cream cheese spread
$\frac{1}{4}$ cup	toasted and chopped walnuts
2-3 cloves	garlic
2 tbsp	olive oil
1 large	red pepper, roasted and peeled

A dash of paprika and salt

To serve

Crusty bread, bread sticks or lavash

METHOD

Process the cream cheese, walnuts, garlic, olive oil and pepper together in a blender till smooth. Transfer to a bowl and add paprika and salt. Chill for 30 minutes and serve with crusty bread, bread sticks or lavash.

Roasted Vegetable Canapés

INGREDIENTS **Serves 6**

2 tbsp	olive oil
3 cloves	garlic, crushed
1 medium	zucchini
1 medium	onion
1 medium	red pepper
1 medium	yellow pepper
½ cup	Hummus (page 233)
6 slices	wholewheat or pita bread
3	cheese slices

A few lettuce leaves
Salt and pepper to taste
A few basil, chopped

To serve
Bottled mustard and chilli flakes

METHOD

Mix the olive oil and garlic together. Cut the vegetables into small cubes. Brush the vegetables with garlic oil and roast them under the grill till soft, but firm. Remove and set aside to cool. Spread hummus on each slice of bread and cut each slice in half diagonally. Cover each triangle with a piece of lettuce to fit the bread. Arrange the vegetables on top and season with salt and pepper. Sprinkle chopped basil and top with a quarter cheese slice. Cook under the grill till the cheese melts. Serve with mustard and chilli flakes.

Rolled Pizza
(Stromboli)

INGREDIENTS

Makes 8-10 appetisers

For the pizza dough

2 tsp	dry yeast
½ tsp	sugar
1 cup	warm water
2½ cups	plain flour
1 tsp	salt
4 tbsp	olive oil + for greasing

For the filling

½ cup	Marinara Sauce (page 232)
1/3 cup	grated mozzarella cheese
½ cup	finely chopped onions
½ cup	finely chopped red or yellow peppers
½ cup	finely chopped olives
1 tbsp	finely chopped basil
1 tsp	dried oregano
1 tsp	chilli flakes

METHOD

For the pizza dough

Sprinkle the yeast and sugar over ¼ cup of lukewarm water. Let it stand for 2-3 minutes, then stir the yeast and sugar mixture until sugar dissolves. Place in a draught free warm place for 5-7 minutes, or until the yeast bubbles up and doubles in volume. Sift flour and salt in a large bowl. Make a well in the centre and pour in the yeast mixture and 2 tbsp oil. Mix the dough with your fingers till you can gather it into a rough ball. Place the dough on a floured board, add 2 tbsp olive oil and knead till smooth and elastic. Dust lightly with flour, place in a bowl, cover and place in a closed oven till double in size.

Preheat the oven to 190°C/375°F/Gas Mark 5. Grease an 8-inch x 12-inch baking sheet with oil. Turn out the risen dough onto a lightly floured surface. Roll and press onto the greased tray. Spread marinara sauce evenly over the dough, leaving a one-inch border along the edges. Sprinkle all the remaining filling ingredients over the sauce. Roll up the dough like a Swiss roll to enclose the filling. Press the edges to seal. Place the Stromboli, joint side down, on the baking sheet. Bake for 20-25 minutes until golden brown and crusty. Cut into slices and serve hot.

Salad-stuffed Baguette

INGREDIENTS **Serves 8-10**

12-14-inch	French bread (baguette)
¼ cup	melted butter
¼ cup	Sour Cream (page 234) or Mayonnaise (page 230)
1 tbsp	chopped fresh herbs
½ cup	crumbled cottage cheese or Cheddar cheese

Salt and pepper to taste

For the salad

1 cup	boiled mixed vegetables (such as broccoli, asparagus, corn kernels)
1 cup	finely chopped vegetables (such as sun-dried tomatoes, spring onions, lettuce leaves, olives, peppers etc.)
2 tbsp	olive oil
2 tbsp	balsamic vinegar
2 tbsp	freshly chopped herbs
2-3 cloves	garlic (optional), crushed

Salt and pepper to taste

METHOD

Cut the bread horizontally in half. Scoop out the soft crumbs to create a hollow space. Brush both sides with butter and warm the bread slightly in an oven. Remove and set aside to cool. Spread sour cream or mayonnaise on the cut sides of both halves. Mix herbs with cottage cheese, salt and peppers and sprinkle all over the base of the bread.

For the salad

In a medium-sized bowl, mix all the ingredients for the salad and toss gently to mix. Spread the salad on the bottom half of the bread. Cover with the top half and press down gently. Wrap the loaf in cling film or foil and refrigerate for 1-2 hours. Remove and cut the loaf vertically in 1-inch thick slices and serve.

Note: You can use 2 cups of any salad for the filling.

Scallion Biscuits

INGREDIENTS **Makes 16 biscuits**

2 cups	plain flour, sieved
1 tbsp	baking powder
1 tsp	salt or garlic salt
6 tbsp	cold butter, cut into cubes
1 cup	finely chopped scallions
¼ cup	finely chopped toasted walnuts
¾ cup + 1 tbsp	milk

To serve

Cream cheese or Sour Cream (page 234)

METHOD

Preheat the oven to 150°C/300°F/Gas Mark 2. Mix together flour, baking powder and salt. Blend in butter with your fingertips until the mixture resembles coarse meal. Add scallions, walnuts and ¾ cup of milk. Mix to make a dough. Turn out the dough onto a lightly floured surface and knead well. Pat the mixture into an 8-inch square tin. Cut into 2-inch square pieces and place on a buttered baking sheet, 1½ inches apart. Brush with remaining of milk and bake for 12-15 minutes until golden. Remove and serve with cream cheese or sour cream.

Note: This also makes a good accompaniment to soups or main courses.

Sesame Tofu with Cucumber-chilli Jelly

INGREDIENTS **Serves 6-8**

For the bean curd

250 gms	bean curd, cut into 12 even-sized cubes
1 tbsp	olive oil
1 tbsp	soy sauce
1 tbsp	mustard
1 tbsp	chopped shallots
1 tbsp	grated ginger
¼ cup	toasted sesame seeds
12	coriander leaves

Salt and pepper to taste

For the cucumber-chilli jelly

1 large	cucumber, peeled and chopped
2 tsp	unflavoured gelatine
1 small	red chilli, chopped
1 tsp	mustard paste

Juice of ½ lemon
Salt to taste

METHOD

For the jelly

Process cucumber in a food processor and strain through a sieve. Mix 2 tablespoons of cucumber juice with gelatine and dissolve over gentle heat. Add the rest of the juice and the jelly ingredients. Pour into a 450 gm loaf tin and freeze until set.

For the bean curd

Toss bean curd cubes in oil. Season and sear on a hot pan or under a hot grill for 1 minute on each side. Add soy, mustard, shallots and ginger. Cover and refrigerate for half an hour. Drain and coat with sesame seeds.

Unmould jelly from the tin and cut into cubes the same size as the bean curd cubes. Arrange the bean curd cubes on a serving platter. Top each piece with a coriander leaf and a cube of jelly. Serve cold.

Spinach and Water Chestnut Dip

INGREDIENTS **Serves 4-6**

1 tbsp	olive oil
1 clove	garlic, finely chopped
1 tsp	dried tarragon
1/2 cup	finely chopped spring onions
2 1/2 cups	washed and chopped spinach
1/2 cup	chopped water chestnuts
1/4 cup	Sour Cream (page 234)
3/4 cup	thick yogurt

Salt, pepper and mustard to taste

To serve
Crackers or crudités (raw vegetables)

Method
Heat oil in a frying pan and fry the garlic, tarragon and spring onions for 2 minutes. Add spinach and water chestnuts and fry briefly. The spinach should be slightly limp. Add seasonings and cook till the water dries up. Remove from heat and set aside to cool completely.

In a small bowl, mix together the sour cream and yogurt. Add cooled spinach mixture and mix well. Transfer to a serving bowl and chill for 1-2 hours. Serve with crackers and crudités.

Spicy Cottage Cheese Tarts

INGREDIENTS

Makes 20 tarts

2 tbsp	oil
1 tsp	cumin seeds
¼ cup	chopped and roasted cashew nuts
1 medium	red pepper, roasted and skin removed
1 medium	green capsicum, roasted and skin removed
2 medium	tomatoes, blanched and cut into small cubes
1 medium	onion, cut into small cubes
1 tsp	dried fenugreek leaves
1 tsp	turmeric powder
2 tbsp	ginger-garlic paste
1 tbsp	red chilli paste
400 gms	cottage cheese, cut into small cubes
20	tart cases
Salt to taste	

To garnish

Finely chopped coriander

METHOD

Heat oil in a frying pan; add the cumin seeds. When they begin to crackle add the cashew nuts and the vegetables and sauté for 1 minute. Add dried fenugreek leaves, turmeric powder, ginger-garlic and chilli pastes and cook for 1 minute. Add cottage cheese cubes and salt. Toss gently to mix and cook until the vegetables are tender but crisp. Remove and allow to cool slightly. Fill each tart case with 1 tablespoon of the mixture, garnish with coriander and serve immediately.

Steamed Cakes of Mixed Greens

Steamed Corn Cakes

Steamed Fenugreek Dumplings

Spicy Cottage Cheese Tarts

South-Western Fries

INGREDIENTS

Serves 4

2 large	potatoes, washed, peeled and cut into finger chips
½ cup	cooking oil

For the South-Western Spice Rub

1 tsp	garlic powder
1 tsp	grated ginger
1 tsp	onion powder
2 tsp	mustard
2 tsp	cumin powder
½ tsp	pepper
2 tsp	dried oregano
3-4 tbsp	vinegar
3-4 tbsp	powdered brown sugar

Salt to taste
Chilli flakes to taste

METHOD

Soak the potato chips in cold water. Mix all the ingredients for the spice rub and set aside. Drain the potatoes and dry them thoroughly. Heat the oil; fry half the potatoes until crisp and drain on kitchen paper. Sprinkle half the spice mixture over the potato chips and toss. Do the same for the other half of potatoes. Serve immediately or transfer to an oven tray and keep warm till ready to serve.

Notes: 1. You can use 250 gms frozen potato chips instead of fresh potato chips.
2. You can make the South-Western Spice Rub and store it in an airtight jar in the refrigerator for later use.

South-Western Tortilla Wedges

INGREDIENTS **Serves 8**

½ cup	Red Salsa (page 234)
¼ cup	finely chopped red pepper
½ cup	Sour Cream (page 234)
6	8-inch round flour tortillas
1 cup	Refried Beans (page 235)
1 cup	shredded Monterey Jack or mozzarella cheese
½ cup	sliced jalapeño chillies

METHOD

Mix together the salsa, red pepper and sour cream. Divide into two portions. Place two tortillas on an ungreased baking sheet and spread with this mixture. Spread two tortillas with refried beans and place them on top of salsa mixture. Spread two more tortillas with the cheese and jalapeños and bake for about 15 minutes or until the cheese has melted. Cut each tortilla into 8 wedges and serve hot.

Spicy Armenian-style Pizzas
(Lahamahjoon)

INGREDIENTS **Serves 8-10**

¾ cup	finely chopped onion
¼ cup	finely chopped red pepper
2 tbsp	olive oil
2 tbsp	finely chopped parsley
1 tsp	dried basil
1 tsp	dried oregano
1 tsp	chopped garlic
1 tsp	chopped mint
½ tsp	cumin powder
200 gms	cottage cheese, cubed and grilled
½ cup	blanched and diced tomatoes
2 tbsp	tomato paste
4	7-inch round pizza bases

Salt, pepper and chilli flakes to taste

METHOD

Sauté the onion and pepper in olive oil till tender. Add parsley, basil, oregano, garlic, mint, cumin, salt, pepper and chilli flakes. Cook for 2 minutes. Add the cottage cheese, tomato and tomato paste. Cover and refrigerate for 2 hours or overnight to marry the flavours. Preheat the oven to 200°C/400°F/Gas Mark 6. Spoon the topping on the pizza base spreading evenly to the edges. Place each one on a baking sheet and bake for 20 minutes. Remove and cut into small wedges and serve hot or cold.

Spinach and Almond Squares

Makes 30-32 squares

INGREDIENTS

For the filling

3 bunches	spinach (400-450 grams), cleaned, boiled and mashed
4 tbsp	Parmesan cheese
4 tbsp	cream cheese
2 tbsp	wholewheat flour, sifted
½ cup	milk
½ tsp	salt
½ tsp	pepper
½ tsp	nutmeg powder

For the pastry

1 cup	plain flour
1 tsp	soda bicarbonate
½ tsp	salt
1 cup	powdered almonds
½ cup	grated Parmesan cheese
¾ cup	melted butter

To serve

Sour Cream (page 234)

METHOD

For the filling

Mix all the ingredients together in a saucepan and cook until all the liquid has dried up. Set aside to cool completely.

For the pastry

Sift together the flour, soda bicarbonate and salt. In a large bowl, combine the flour mixture with almonds and Parmesan cheese. Make a well in the centre and add the melted butter. Make a soft dough, using your fingertips. Refrigerate the dough for

10 minutes. Remove and roll out half the dough in a rectangle shape to fit the base of a 13 inch x 9 inch Swiss roll tin. Spread the mashed spinach evenly over the dough. Roll out the remaining dough and cover the spinach mixture. Seal the edges. Bake in a hot oven at 150°C/300°F/Gas Mark 2 for 25-30 minutes. Remove and allow the pastry to cool for 5-7 minutes. Cut into 1-inch squares and serve warm with sour cream.

Spicy Cottage Cheese Wraps

INGREDIENTS

Serves 6

250 gms	cottage cheese, cut into 1-inch cubes
1 medium	green or red pepper, cut into 1-inch cubes
1 medium	onion, cut into 1-inch cubes
1 medium	tomato, deseeded and cut into 1-inch cubes
3 tbsp	oil
2-3 tbsp	tandoori paste
1 tbsp	red chilli paste
1 medium	onion, grated
¼ cup	tomato purée
1 cup	yogurt, beaten
3 large	warm Roomali Rotis (page 92)
Salt to taste	

To serve

Sliced onions, chopped fresh coriander, lemon wedges and Green Chutney (page 236)

METHOD

Mix together the cottage cheese and vegetables in a large bowl. In a frying pan, heat 2 tablespoons oil and add the tandoori paste, chilli paste and grated onion. Fry for 3-4 minutes. Add tomato purée, salt and yogurt and mix well. Remove from heat and pour over the cottage cheese and vegetables. Cover and set aside to marinate for 45 minutes or more. Grease a frying pan or an ovenproof dish with 1 tablespoon of oil. Either sauté the cottage cheese and the vegetables or grill till golden brown. To serve, place each warmed roomali roti on a flat surface and spoon 1/3 of the mixture on one end of the roti. Roll up the roti, folding in the ends as you roll. Serve immediately with sliced onions, coriander, lemon wedges and green chutney.

Note: Tandoori paste can be replaced with 2 tablespoons of tandoori masala and 1 tablespoon of garam masala.

Spicy Crumbled Lentil Cakes
(Amiri Khaman)

Serves ....

INGREDIENTS

200 gms	packaged khaman dhokla mix or
250 gms	khaman dhokla
1 tbsp	sugar
1 tbsp	lemon juice

For the tempering

3 tbsp	oil
3 tbsp	raisins
3 tbsp	broken cashew nuts
1 tsp	mustard seeds
1 tsp	sesame seeds
½ tsp	asafoetida
6-8 cloves	garlic, crushed
2-3	green chillies, chopped

A few curry leaves

To garnish

Grated coconut, chopped coriander and fine sev

METHOD

Prepare dhokla according to the directions on the packet. Set aside to cool. Crumble the dhokla. Add sugar and lemon juice, mix well and set aside. Heat oil in a pan; add mustard and sesame seeds. When they splutter, add asafoetida, garlic, chillies and curry leaves. Fry briefly and add cashew pieces and raisins. Cook until golden brown but not burnt. Add to the crumbled dhokla and mix well. Transfer to a serving bowl and garnish with coconut, coriander and sev. Serve warm.

Spicy Party Dip

INGREDIENTS

Serves 8

1/3 cup	chopped almonds
1 tbsp	melted butter
200 gms	cream cheese, softened
1/3 cup	grated processed cheese
2 tbsp	taco seasoning
2-3	spring onion stems, finely chopped
½ cup	Red Salsa (page 234)

Salt to taste

To serve

Crackers or corn chips

METHOD

Toast almonds lightly in the oven. Remove and stir in butter and salt. Mix together the cream cheese, grated cheese, taco seasoning, spring onion and salsa. Stir in the almonds and pour the mixture into an 8-inch square tin. Bake in a hot oven until thoroughly heated. Serve with crackers or chips.

Spicy Pinwheels

INGREDIENTS **Makes 40 appetisers**

½ cup	finely chopped jalapeño chillies
½ cup	finely chopped red pepper
2	spring onion stems, finely chopped
¼ cup	chopped black olives
3 tbsp	chopped coriander leaves
3 tbsp	hot sauce
180-200 gms	cream cheese, softened
8	10-inch flour tortillas

Salt to taste
Taco tempering to taste

To serve
Red Salsa (page 234)

METHOD

In a small bowl, mix together all the ingredients except tortillas. Spread a quarter cup of the mixture over each tortilla and roll up tightly like a Swiss roll. Arrange all the rolls on a plate, cover with cling film and chill for 1 hour. Remove and cut each one into ½-inch thick slices. Serve pinwheels with the salsa.

Spicy Bean Salsa

INGREDIENTS **Serves 6**

For the Salsa

½ cup	black-eyed beans
½ cup	black beans
½ cup	boiled or tinned corn kernels
¼ cup	finely chopped onion,
¼ cup	finely chopped tomato
¼ cup	finely chopped green capsicum
2 tbsp	finely chopped jalapeño chillies
1 tbsp	finely chopped coriander

For the dressing

2 tbsp	vinegar
2 tbsp	water
2 tbsp	olive oil
½ tsp	dried oregano
½ tsp	black pepper
½ tsp	dried garlic powder
½ tsp	salt
½ tsp	sugar
1 tsp	taco seasoning
1 tsp	red chilli paste

To serve

Taco chips

METHOD

Soak the beans overnight and boil till tender. Place all the ingredients for the dressing in a jar and shake until well blended. In a medium bowl, mix all the ingredients for the salsa and add the dressing. Adjust salt. Cover and store in the refrigerator overnight, or for at least six hours, for the flavours to blend. Serve with taco chips.

Spinach and Artichoke Pie

INGREDIENTS **Serves 6-8**

1 cup	fresh cream
1 tbsp	plain flour
½ tsp	garlic salt and pepper mixed together
4 tbsp	Parmesan cheese
400 gms	spinach leaves, chopped, blanched and drained
1 cup	grated Cheddar or Gouda cheese
1 tin (400 gms)	artichoke hearts, drained and chopped
¼ cup	slivered and re-hydrated sun-dried tomatoes

To serve

Thinly sliced and toasted bread

METHOD

Preheat the oven to 180°C/350°F/Gas Mark 4. In a glass bowl, mix together cream, flour, garlic salt-pepper mixture and 2 tablespoons of Parmesan cheese. Heat gently in a microwave oven or in a small saucepan over medium heat. Cook until slightly thick, stirring all the time. Stir in the spinach, cheese, artichoke hearts and sun-dried tomatoes. Turn the mixture out into a 9-inch pie dish and spread evenly. Bake for 15-18 minutes or until hot and bubbly. Serve with toasted bread.

Spinach and Cream Cheese Tacos

INGREDIENTS **Serves 8**

1 tbsp	olive oil
½ cup	finely chopped spring onions
1 tbsp	crushed garlic
1 cup	puréed spinach
½ cup	cream cheese
¼ cup	grated Monterey Jack cheese
1-2 tbsp	finely chopped jalapeño chillies
6-8 small	taco shells

Salt, pepper and nutmeg to taste

METHOD

Heat olive oil in a frying pan; sauté spring onions and garlic until soft. Add spinach and cook until the mixture is dry. Remove from heat and cool the mixture slightly. Add the cream cheese, salt, pepper and nutmeg. Cool the mixture completely. Preheat the oven to 180°C/350°F/Gas Mark 4. Mix together the grated cheese and jalapeño chillies and toss gently. Spoon 2 tablespoons of the spinach mixture in each taco shell, sprinkle the cheese and jalapeño mixture on top and bake for 5-7 minutes. Serve right away.

Sun-dried Tomato and Pesto Torta

INGREDIENTS

Makes 20

4 cloves	garlic
1½ cups	fresh basil leaves
¼ cup	pine nuts
2 tbsp	olive oil
1 tsp	fresh lemon juice
2 2/3 cups	cream cheese at room temperature
¼ cup	Parmesan cheese
1cups	sun-dried tomatoes, soaked in hot water
1 1/3 cup	tomato paste
¾ cup	butter at room temperature

Salt and pepper to taste

To garnish

Fresh basil sprigs and toasted pine nuts

To serve

Toasted French bread (baguette) slices

METHOD

Finely chop the garlic in a food processor. Add basil, pine nuts, oil and lemon juice. Process until well blended. Add one-third cup cream cheese and one-fourth cup Parmesan cheese. Using on/off turns, process just until blended. Transfer the pesto to a medium bowl.

Chop the tomatoes coarsely in the processor. Add tomato paste and process until the mixture is almost smooth. Add one-third cup cream cheese and blend well. Using an electric mixer, beat 2 cups of cream cheese and butter in a large bowl until fluffy. Season with salt and pepper.

Grease a 6-cup capacity dish or tin with oil and line it with cling film, extending the film over the sides. Spread three-fourth cup cream cheese-butter mixture evenly over the bottom of the prepared dish. Top with half the tomato mixture, then half cup cream cheese-butter mixture, followed by half the pesto mixture. Repeat the layers with half cup cream cheese-butter mixture, remaining tomato mixture, half cup cream cheese-butter mixture and remaining pesto. Top with the remaining cream cheese-butter mixture. Cover and chill overnight. To serve, invert the torta onto a platter. Peel off the cling film and garnish with basil sprigs and toasted pine nuts. Serve with baguette slices.

Note: The torta can be made 3 days ahead and kept refrigerated.

Spinach Brownies

INGREDIENTS **Makes 16 brownies**

4 bunches (750-800 gms)	spinach leaves, rinsed and chopped
1 cup	plain flour
1 tsp	baking powder
1 tsp	salt
1 tsp	pepper
1 cup	milk
½ cup	thick cream
½ cup	softened butter
1 small	onion, finely chopped
1 cup	grated mozzarella cheese
2-3 tbsp	toasted and chopped pine nuts

Butter for greasing

To garnish

Grated Parmesan cheese

To serve

Sour Cream (page 234) or cream cheese

METHOD

Preheat the oven to 190°C/375°F/Gas Mark 5. Lightly grease an 8-inch square tin with butter. Place spinach in a medium saucepan with enough water to cover. Bring to a boil. Lower the heat and cook for about 3 minutes until spinach is limp. Remove from heat and set aside. In a large bowl, mix flour, baking powder, salt and pepper. Stir in the milk, cream and butter. Mix in the spinach, onion, cheese and pine nuts and transfer the mixture to the prepared tin. Bake for 30-35 minutes or until a toothpick inserted in the centre comes out clean. Cool slightly and sprinkle with Parmesan cheese. Cut into 2-inch squares. Remove from the pan and serve warm with sour cream or cream cheese.

Spinach Crisps with Gram Noodles
(Palak Sev Puri)

INGREDIENTS

Serves 4

15-20	spinach leaves, washed and cut into 2-inch circles
2 medium	potatoes, cubed and boiled
1 small	onion, finely chopped
½ cup	Sweet and Sour Chutney (page 236)
½ cup	Garlic Chutney (page 236)

Oil for deep-frying

For the batter

¼ cup	gram flour
¼ cup	water
½ tsp	salt
½ tsp	chilli powder
½ tsp	lemon juice
½ tsp	carom seeds

A pinch of asafoetida
A pinch of fruit salt

To garnish

½ cup	fine sev

Finely chopped fresh coriander

METHOD

Mix all the ingredients for the batter and beat until smooth. Set aside for 30 minutes. Drain spinach leaves and dip each one in the prepared batter and deep-fry in hot oil, 2-3 at a time, until crisp. Drain on kitchen paper and allow to cool. Arrange 5-6 fried spinach puries on a plate. Place 3-4 potato cubes on each one followed by chopped onion. Drizzle with both the chutneys to taste. Sprinkle sev and coriander leaves and serve right away.

Sprouted Green Bean Dumplings in Yogurt (Hara Moong Dahi Vada)

INGREDIENTS Serves 6-8

½ cup	yellow lentils, soaked for 6 hours
½ cup	white lentils, soaked for 6 hours
2 tbsp	ginger-chilli paste
1 large	potato, boiled and mashed
½ cup	sprouted green beans, boiled
½ tsp	garam masala
½ tsp	chilli powder
1 tsp	sugar

Salt to taste
Juice of ½ a lemon
Oil for deep-frying

To garnish

2 cups beaten yogurt, Sweet and Sour Chutney (page 236), salt, roasted cumin powder, chilli powder fine sev, and 2 tbsp finely chopped coriander.

METHOD

Mix both the lentils and grind into a fine paste without much water. Add salt and ginger-chilli paste. Set aside. Mix mashed potato with boiled green beans. Add garam masala, chilli powder, salt, sugar and lemon juice. Mix well. Form walnut-sized balls of the mixture. Heat oil till it begins to smoke. Dip potato and beans balls into the lentil mixture to coat thickly. Deep-fry in hot oil till golden brown. Remove from oil and drop the balls in a bowl of water. Soak for 5-7 minutes. Remove from water and squeeze to remove excess water. Place on a serving platter. Top the dumplings with beaten yogurt. Garnish with sweet-sour chutney, salt, cumin powder, chilli powder, fine sev and coriander. Serve cold.

Steamed Cakes of Mixed Greens
(Bhaji na Muthia)

INGREDIENTS **Serves 6**

1 cup	wheat flour
1/4 cup	black millet flour
1/4 cup	white millet flour
1 tbsp	semolina
1 tbsp	gram flour
2 cups	mixed greens (fenugreek, spinach and other greens)
2 tbsp	ginger-chilli paste
2 tbsp	oil
2 tbsp	yogurt
1 tsp	sugar
1 tsp	sesame seeds

1 tsp salt

A pinch of soda bicarbonate

For the tempering

1-2 tbsp	oil
1/2 tsp	mustard seeds
1/2 tsp	sesame seeds
1/2 tsp	asafoetida

A few curry leaves

To garnish

Grated fresh coconut and chopped coriander leaves

To serve

Green Chutney (page 236)

METHOD

In a large bowl, mix together all the flours and semolina. Add the remaining ingredients and knead into a very soft dough. Divide the dough into 2 or 3 parts and roll into cylindrical shapes. Place the rolls in a greased perforated steamer tray. Cover and steam for 30 minutes. Remove and set aside to cool. Cut each roll into half-inch slices. For the tempering, heat the oil in a frying pan; add the mustard and sesame seeds. When they begin to crackle, add the asafoetida and curry leaves. Place the sliced dumplings over the sizzling spices in the pan and heat them through. Turn over and cook the other side as well. Transfer to a serving plate, garnish with grated coconut and chopped coriander and serve hot with green chutney.

Steamed Corn Cakes
(Makkai na Dhokla)

INGREDIENTS **Serves 6-8**

1 cup	corn kernels, boiled
2 cups	ready-mixed idli batter
2 tbsp	chopped ginger-chilli paste
½ tsp	turmeric powder
Salt to taste	
Oil for greasing	

To serve

Coconut Chutney (page 236)

METHOD

Mix the boiled corn into the idli batter. Add the chopped ginger-chilli paste, turmeric and salt. Divide the batter into 2 parts. Grease two 8-inch round metal plates with oil. Bring some water to boil in a steamer. Mix the powder in the sachet which accompanies the idli batter, with a little water. Add this to the batter. Immediately pour the batter into the prepared plates and steam as for dhoklas. Remove the steamed batter, cool for 5 minutes, cut into small square pieces and serve with coconut chutney.

Steamed Fenugreek Dumplings
(Methi Dhokla)

INGREDIENTS

Makes 30 pieces

500 gms	khaman dhokla mix
½ cup	fenugreek leaves, finely chopped
1 tbsp	oil + to grease the pan
2 tsp	ginger-chilli paste

For the tempering

2-3 tbsp	oil
1 tsp	mustard seeds
¼ tsp	asafoetida
2-3	green chillies

A few curry leaves

To garnish

Coriander leaves and grated coconut

To serve

Coconut Chutney (page 236)

METHOD

Empty the contents of the packet in a large bowl. Mix fenugreek leaves, the contents of the small sachet, which comes with the dhokla packet, oil and 1½ cups water. Mix thoroughly and spoon it into the greased idli mould and steam it in a covered vessel over hot water for 15 minutes. Remove with a sharp knife and place it in a serving dish.

For the tempering

Heat oil in a small pan; add mustard seeds and asafoetida followed by curry leaves and chopped green chillies.

Drizzle the tempering over the dhoklas. Garnish with coriander and grated coconut and serve hot with coconut chutney.

Steamed Mangalore Spiced Cakes
(Mangalore Masala Idlis)

INGREDIENTS **Makes 10-12 regular or 20-24 cocktail idlis**

¼ cup	grated coconut
2-3	dried red chillies
1 tbsp	tamarind pulp
2 cups	ready-mixed idli batter
2-3	Madras onions, chopped
1 tsp	sugar
1 tbsp	oil + for greasing
1 tsp	soda bicarbonate
Salt to taste	

To serve

Butter or Malgapudi Chutney

METHOD

Make a paste with grated coconut, red chillies and tamarind pulp. Add to the idli batter and mix well. Fold in chopped onions, sugar, salt and oil. Heat some water in a steamer. Grease idli moulds. When the water begins to boil, mix soda bicarbonate in a little water and add to the idli batter. Spoon batter into the moulds and steam for 15 minutes. Remove from moulds and serve hot with butter or Malgapudi chutney.

Sun-dried Tomato and Basil Wrap

INGREDIENTS **Makes 12-14**

For the wraps

1 cup	plain flour
1 tbsp	sun-dried tomato paste
1 tsp	dried basil
1 tsp	garlic salt
1 tsp	paprika

For the filling

1 medium	tomato, blanched, deseeded and chopped
½ cup	cream cheese spread or crumbled feta cheese
1 cup	Hummus (page 233)

A few lettuce leaves, sliced onions and chopped jalapeño chillies

To serve

Sour Cream (page 234) or ranch dressing

METHOD

Knead all the ingredients for the wraps into a soft dough. Divide the dough into 12-14 portions. Roll out each portion into a 3-inch round and roast both sides on a hot dry griddle. Set aside.

For the filling

Mix together chopped tomato, cream cheese or feta cheese and hummus.

Spread 1-2 tablespoons of hummus-cheese mixture evenly on each wrap. Arrange lettuce, onions and jalapeños on top. Roll up and serve with ranch dressing or sour cream.

Vegetable Juliennes with Red Pepper Coulis

INGREDIENTS Serves 4

500 gms	mixed vegetables (carrots, snow peas, asparagus, broccoli, cauliflower etc)
2	bay leaves

Sprigs of fresh thyme

For the red pepper coulis

1 small	onion, chopped
1 clove	garlic, crushed
1 tbsp	olive oil
3 medium	red peppers, roasted, peeled and chopped
8 tbsp	fresh cream

Juice of 1 lemon

Salt and pepper to taste

To garnish

Fresh herbs

METHOD

Cut the vegetables into finger lengths and steam over boiling salted water to which bay leaves and thyme sprigs have been added.

For the red pepper coulis

Sauté onion and garlic in olive oil and 1 tablespoon of water for 3 minutes in a thick-bottomed frying pan. Add chopped red peppers and cook for 2 more minutes. Remove from heat and process in a blender. Transfer to a bowl and add the cream, lemon juice, salt and pepper. Keep warm.

Arrange steamed vegetables on a platter and pour the coulis on one side. Garnish with fresh herbs and serve warm.

Three Split Gram Cakes

Vegetable Juliennes with Red Pepper Coulis

Sun-dried Tomato and Feta Cheese Marinade

INGREDIENTS **Makes 250 gms**

1 tsp	crushed garlic
1 tsp	mixed dried herbs
1 tsp	salt
1 tsp	pepper
1 tsp	chilli flakes
1 tsp	balsamic vinegar
1/4 cup	sun-dried tomatoes, cut into 1/4-inch cubes
1/4 cup	black or green olives, sliced
1/4 cup	feta cheese, cut into 1/4-inch cubes
1/2-3/4 cup	olive oil

METHOD

Wash and wipe completely dry a 2-cup capacity glass jar. In a small bowl, mix together garlic, herbs, salt, pepper, chilli flakes and balsamic vinegar. Layer sun-dried tomatoes, olives and feta cheese one by one in the jar. Repeat the layers till the jar is three-fourth full. Pour olive oil till the top. Close tightly and place in the refrigerator to marinate for 2-3 days.

This marinade can be used for various dishes :

1. As a dressing pour 1-2 tablespoons over a green salad.
2. As a topping on crostini.
3. On pasta - add 2-3 tablespoons and toss.
4. Spoon 1 tablespoon into a lettuce leaf cup and serve as a starter.

Warm Mushroom Dip
Wonton Cups
Thai Peanut Dip
Sun-dried Tomato and Feta Cheese Marinade

Spinach and Water Chestnut Canapés

INGREDIENTS **Makes 14**

1 tbsp	olive oil
1 tbsp	butter
1 clove	garlic, minced
½ cup	finely chopped spring onions
2½ cups	spinach, washed and chopped
½ cup	finely chopped water chestnuts
½ cup	whipping cream
½ cup	thick yogurt
2 tbsp	lemon juice
12-14	tart cases or bread cut into 2-inch squares

Salt, pepper and nutmeg to taste

To garnish

Toasted pine nuts

METHOD

Heat olive oil and butter in a frying pan; fry garlic and spring onions for 2 minutes. Add spinach and water chestnuts and fry briefly. The spinach should be slightly limp. Cook further till the water dries up. Add salt, pepper and nutmeg. Remove from heat and allow to cool completely. In a small bowl, whip the cream, fold in the thick yogurt, salt and lemon juice. Add the cooled spinach mixture and mix well. Transfer to a serving bowl and chill for 1-2 hours. Fill each tart case with 1 tablespoon of the mixture, garnish with toasted pine nuts and serve at once. Alternatively, spoon the mixture onto the bread squares, garnish and serve.

Sushi Rolls
(Hosamaki)

Serves 6-8

INGREDIENTS

1 cup	sushi rice
2 cups	water
2 tbsp	rice vinegar dressing
2 tbsp	black sesame seeds
½ tsp	salt
2 tbsp	sugar
4	8-inch x 7-inch nori sheets

For the filling

1 medium	cucumber, peeled, thinly sliced and salted
2 tbsp	sliced pickled ginger
3 tbsp	pickled radish

Thin strips of egg omelette
Thin strips of avocado

To serve

Kikkoman soy sauce, wasabi paste, pickled ginger and togarashi

METHOD

Cook the rice in boiling water until all the water has been absorbed. Cover and set aside for 10 minutes. In a small pan, mix vinegar, sesame seeds, salt and sugar and cook over low heat. Cool to room temperature over a bowl of iced water. Toss rice and vinegar dressing with a wooden spoon on a cutting board. Do not add all the dressing as the rice will get mushy. Add as much dressing as the rice can absorb. Cover with a damp cloth and set aside.

Toast each nori sheet on an open flame and moisten with water. Place on a bamboo mat. Spread one-fourth of the rice on three-fourth of the nori sheet leaving a 1 to 2-inch border. In the centre of the rice, place any of the filling ingredients. Lift the mat and roll once to make a sushi log. Slightly squeeze along entire roll. Lift the mat and roll again tightly till you get to the end of the sheet. The roll should be tight with the filling in the centre. Use a sharp knife to slice into half-inch rolls. Place the rolls on a flat plate and serve with soy sauce, wasabi paste, pickled ginger and togarashi.

Alternatively, place the toasted and dampened nori sheet on a cutting board. Spread one-fourth of the rice on the nori sheet and spread evenly. At one end of the sheet, place long strips of the chosen fillings; lift the nori sheet and roll up Swiss-roll fashion. Make sure the roll is tight. Cut in half-inch rolls and serve with soy sauce, wasabi paste, pickled ginger and togarashi.

Sun-dried Tomato and Pine Nut Fondue

INGREDIENTS

Serves 4

1 cup	grated Swiss or fondue cheese
1 tbsp	cornflour
1 tbsp	butter
¼ cup	sun-dried tomatoes, soaked in hot water and chopped
1 tbsp	finely chopped garlic
2 tbsp	toasted and chopped pine nuts
¾ cup	Vegetable Stock (page 166)
½ cup	milk

Salt and pepper to taste
A dash of balsamic vinegar

To serve

Cubes of toasted French bread or boiled baby potatoes

METHOD

Toss the cheese in cornflour and set aside. Melt butter in a fondue dish or a thick bottomed saucepan; sauté sun-dried tomato and garlic for 1 minute. Add the pine nuts along with the stock and milk. Bring to a boil and gradually add the cheese mixture, a little at a time, stirring after each addition in figure of 8 movements. This way you make sure that the mixture doesn't stick to the bottom of the dish. Season with salt and pepper and a dash of balsamic vinegar. Simmer the fondue until thick. Serve hot in a fondue dish over a low heat with bread cubes and baby potatoes.

Sweet Pepper Relish with Potato Discs

INGREDIENTS **Serves 6**

For the relish

1 medium	red pepper, finely diced
1 medium	green pepper, finely diced
1 medium	yellow pepper, finely diced
1 small	onion, finely diced
¼ cup	finely chopped green or black olives
1-2 tbsp	balsamic vinegar
1/3 cup	olive oil
1 tbsp	finely chopped fresh mixed herbs
1-2 cloves	garlic, crushed

Salt and pepper to taste

For the potatoes

4-5 medium	potatoes, parboiled, peeled and sliced
2 tbsp	melted butter or olive oil + for greasing
1 tbsp	mixed dried herbs

Salt and pepper to taste

METHOD

For the relish

Mix all the ingredients in a bowl; cover and leave to marinate for 1-2 hours. Pour off excess oil from the top. The oil can be used later to make a vinaigrette dressing or in cooking. Place the pepper mixture in a bowl and serve at room temperature or chilled.

For the potatoes

Preheat the oven to 180°C/350°F/Gas Mark 4. Arrange the sliced potatoes on a greased baking dish and sprinkle salt, pepper and herbs over them. Bake for 10-15 minutes or till golden brown. Serve the potato discs with the pepper relish.

Swiss Tomato Fondue Dip

INGREDIENTS **Serves 4-6**

½ tsp	butter
1 clove	garlic
1 cup	tomato juice
2 cups	grated Swiss cheese (Emmental or Gruyère)
½ tsp	salt
1½ tbsp	cornflour
½ tsp	Worcestershire sauce
½ tsp	pepper
½ tsp	Tabasco sauce
1 tsp	freshly chopped basil
½ tsp	dried oregano

To serve

Thinly sliced French bread, toasted

METHOD

Melt butter in a fondue dish. Add the garlic clove and crush it with a fork. Fry for 1 minute. Add the tomato juice and cook over a low heat for a few minutes. In a large bowl, mix together lightly the grated cheese, salt and cornflour. Add the mixture to the boiling tomato juice, little at a time, stirring well after each addition. When all the cheese has melted, add the Worcestershire sauce, pepper, Tabasco, basil and oregano. Mix thoroughly and cook for 1 minute. Serve at once with toast.

Tahitian Sunset Roll-ups

INGREDIENTS **Makes 12 portions**

250 gms	cottage cheese, cut into 2-inch strips
1 cup	yogurt
2 tsp	curry powder
2 tsp	crushed garlic
½ tsp	salt
2 tbsp	oil
½ cup	fresh coconut flakes
12	iceberg lettuce leaves, soaked in cold water and drained

For the Tahitian dip

1 cup	Sour Cream (page 234)
2 tbsp	finely chopped peanuts
¼ cup	bottled mango relish

METHOD

Marinate cottage cheese strips in a mixture of yogurt, curry powder, garlic and salt. Cover and set aside for 1 hour. Remove the cottage cheese from the yogurt and shallow-fry in oil till golden brown. Remove and set aside. In the same frying pan, roast the coconut flakes lightly and set aside.

Take one lettuce leaf, place a few fried cottage cheese strips at one end of the leaf. Fold both ends of the lettuce leaf over the cheese strips and roll up. Secure with a wooden toothpick. Refrigerate for 1 hour.

For the Tahitian dip

Mix all the three ingredients together in a bowl.

To serve, dip the cheese roll into the dip and then into the coconut flakes and arrange on a plate.

Tender Millet Pancakes
(Ponk na Chilla)

INGREDIENTS **Serves 6-8**

1 cup	split green gram, soaked
2 tbsp	finely chopped green garlic with leaves
1 tbsp	ginger-chilli paste
1 tbsp	chopped coriander
½ cup	Fresh tender millet

Salt to taste
Oil for cooking

To serve

Green Chutney (page 236) mixed with a little yogurt

METHOD

Grind the soaked green gram to a fine paste. Add garlic, ginger-chilli paste, coriander and salt. Heat a griddle and spread ½ teaspoon oil. Pour 2-3 tablespoons of green gram mixture and spread evenly into a thick pancake with the back of a spoon. Immediately sprinkle 1-2 tablespoons of millet all around. Cover and cook for 2-3 minutes. Turn over and cook again for 2 minutes. Transfer to a serving plate, millet side up. Serve hot with green chutney mixed with a little yogurt.

Tex-Mex Wontons

INGREDIENTS **Makes 16 wontons**

½ cup	cream cheese
½ cup	grated Monterey Jack cheese
½ cup	finely chopped jalapeño chillies
3	spring onion stems, finely chopped
2 cloves	garlic, crushed
1 tsp	taco sesoning
16	wonton wrappers

Oil for deep-frying

To serve

Tomato-chilli sauce

METHOD

In a bowl, mix together the cream cheese, Monterey Jack cheese, jalapeño chillies, spring onions, garlic and taco sesoning. Spread this mixture in a tray and place in a freezer to set for approximately 2 hours. Remove the tray from the freezer and cut the mixture into cubes. Place one cube in the centre of each wonton wrapper and fold the wrapper into a triangle bringing the two ends together to form a hat like shape. Stick the ends with a little water. Deep-fry in hot oil until crisp and drain on kitchen paper. Serve with tomato-chilli sauce.

Thai Peanut Dip

INGREDIENTS **Makes 1½ cups**

1 tbsp	sesame oil
2 cloves	garlic, crushed
½ inch	ginger or galangal, crushed
1 tbsp	red chilli paste
1 cup	thick coconut milk
1 tsp	cornflour
1/3 cup	roasted powdered peanuts
1 tbsp	raw sugar
1 tbsp	soy sauce

Salt to taste

To garnish

A few sprigs of coriander and sliced lime leaves

To serve

Crisp fried wonton chips and assorted vegetable crudités (capsicum strips, snow peas, baby corn etc.)

METHOD

Heat oil in a pan and fry garlic, ginger or galangal and chilli paste until fragrant. Add coconut milk mixed with cornflour and the peanuts and bring to a boil. Add sugar, soy sauce and salt and cook until thick. Remove from heat and set aside to cool. Transfer to a serving bowl, garnish with coriander and lime leaves. Serve warm with wonton chips and vegetables.

Thai-style Lettuce Wraps
(Mien Cum)

INGREDIENTS **Serves 6**

1 tbsp	sesame oil
2 tbsp	finely chopped ginger
2 tbsp	finely chopped garlic
2 tbsp	finely chopped red chillies
2 tbsp	finely chopped lemon grass
½ cup	chopped onions
½ cup	chopped fresh mushrooms
¼ cup	finely chopped green capsicum
¼ cup	finely chopped spring onion
½ cup	toasted coconut flakes
½ cup	roasted and crushed peanuts
½ cup	grated unripe green mango
2 tbsp	finely chopped coriander leaves
1 large head	iceberg lettuce
Salt to taste	

For the sauce

¼ cup	powdered peanuts
2 tbsp	brown sugar
1 tsp	soya sauce
1 tsp	chilli sauce
1 tbsp	vinegar
¼ cup	water
Salt to taste	

To serve

1 cup boiled and fried rice noodles

METHOD

For the sauce

Mix all the ingredients together in a saucepan and heat till the sugar has dissolved and mixture is thick. Pour into a serving bowl and set aside.

Heat oil in a frying pan; fry ginger, garlic, red chillies, lemon grass and onion until soft. Add the remaining ingredients, except the lettuce and cook on a high heat. Keep the mixture warm on a sizzler plate.

To serve

Fold each lettuce leaf into a cup shape. Place a spoonful of mixture in the cup, top with a teaspoon of the sauce and sprinkle crushed fried noodles on top.

Three Split Gram Cakes
(Trevati Daal na Dhokla)

INGREDIENTS — **Makes 30-35**

½ cup	yellow split gram
½ cup	skinless split black gram
½ cup	Bengal split gram
3 tbsp	sour yogurt
1 tbsp	sugar
1 tbsp	ginger-chilli paste
2 tbsp	oil
2 tbsp	lemon juice
1 tsp	soda bicarbonate
1 tsp	fruit salt

Oil for greasing
Salt to taste

For the tempering

2 tbsp	oil
1 tsp	mustard seeds

A pinch of asafoetida
A few curry leaves

To garnish

Finely chopped coriander and grated fresh coconut

To serve

Green Chutney (page 236)

METHOD

24 hours before you plan to make the dhokla, soak all the legumes for 6-8 hours. Drain. Grind to a thick paste, transfer into a large container and add sour yogurt and sugar. Mix well. Add enough warm water to get a dropping consistency. Cover and set aside for 6-8 hours so that the batter ferments. When you want to make the dhokla, place a wide pan filled with water on heat. Place a metal ring in the centre of the pan. Cover and bring the water to a boil. Grease a 9-inch stainless steel round plate with oil and place it on the ring above the water.

In the meanwhile, lightly mix the fermented batter. Add ginger-chilli paste, salt and oil. In a small bowl, mix lemon juice with soda bicarbonate and fruit salt. Gently fold the mixture into the batter. Pour the batter immediately into the prepared steel plate. Cover and steam for 30-35 minutes. To check if the dhokla is ready, insert a knife through the centre. If it comes out clean, the dhokla is cooked. Remove from heat and set aside. Cut the dhokla into squares.

For the tempering

In a small pan, heat oil and add mustard seeds. When they begin to crackle, add the asafoetida and curry leaves. Remove from heat and sprinkle over the steamed dhoklas. Garnish with coriander and grated coconut and serve hot or warm with green chutney.

Toasted Asparagus Rolls

INGREDIENTS **Serves 8**

8	thick fresh or tinned asparagus spears
100 gms	butter, softened
1 tbsp	coarse-grained mustard
8 slices	Cheddar cheese
8	thin white bread slices

Grated rind of one lemon
Salt and pepper to taste

METHOD

Preheat the oven to 190°C/375°F/Gas Mark 5. If using fresh asparagus, blanch them in boiling salted water till just tender. If using tinned ones, drain all the water and place them on a plate to dry. In a small bowl, blend two-thirds of the butter with the mustard, lemon rind, salt and pepper. Spread this mixture on the bread slices. Press 1 slice of cheese on each slice of bread. Place 1 asparagus spear at the edge of each bread slice and roll it up lightly. Secure the edge with a toothpick. Place the rolls joint side down on a lightly greased baking sheet. Melt the remaining butter and brush over the rolls. Bake for 12-15 minutes till golden brown. Cool slightly before serving.

Tofu Satay with Peanut Sauce

INGREDIENTS **Serves 4-6**

1 cup	coconut milk
½ tbsp	curry powder
½ tsp	salt
200 gms	tofu, cut into 1-inch x 2-inch pieces

For the peanut sauce

2	1-inch long lemon grass pieces, sliced
1 tbsp	chopped galangal
2 tbsp	chopped shallots
2 tbsp	garlic
6-8	dried red chillies
1 cup	coconut milk
2 tbsp	tamarind pulp
1 cup	roasted crushed peanuts
1 tbsp	soy sauce
2 tbsp	raw sugar

Salt to taste

METHOD

Mix together coconut milk, curry powder and salt. Soak tofu pieces in the mixture for 30 minutes. Thread onto skewers or bamboo sticks and grill over a charcoal fire or under an electric grill. Serve hot with peanut sauce.

For the peanut sauce

Make a smooth paste of lemon grass, galangal, shallots, garlic and chillies using a mortar and pestle. In a small saucepan; heat coconut milk gently. Add the paste, salt, tamarind pulp, peanuts, soy sauce and sugar. Cook until thick. Remove from heat and set aside to cool. Serve with the grilled tofu.

Tortilla Spring Rolls

INGREDIENTS **Makes 12 pieces**

1½ cups	mixed shredded cabbage and bean sprouts
2	spring onion stems, finely chopped
¼ cup	water chestnuts or fresh button mushrooms, chopped
2-3 tbsp	powdered peanuts
3 tbsp	plum sauce
1 tsp	sesame oil
3	6-inch tortillas

Salt and pepper to taste

To serve
Sweet chilli sauce

METHOD

In a medium bowl, combine cabbage, bean sprouts, spring onion, water chestnuts or mushrooms, powdered peanuts, 2 tablespoons of plum sauce and oil. Add salt and pepper and mix well. Spread the remaining plum sauce evenly on each tortilla. Spread half a cup of vegetable mixture on each tortilla, a quarter inch inside the edge. Roll up the tortillas and wrap tightly in plastic wrap. Refrigerate for at least one hour. Cut each tortilla roll into 4 pieces and serve with sweet chilli sauce.

Vegetable Dip

INGREDIENTS **Makes 1¼ cups**

½ cup	cottage cheese
½ cup	Sour Cream (page 234)
¼ cup	finely chopped cucumber
¼ cup	finely chopped spring onion
¼ cup	finely chopped celery
¼ cup	finely chopped radish
½ tsp	garlic salt
¼ tsp	pepper
1 tbsp	chopped chives
2 tbsp	olive oil

To serve

Potato skins, pita bread triangles or crisp lettuce leaves

METHOD

Blend cottage cheese and sour cream in a bowl and add the rest of the ingredients. Cover and chill. Serve with potato skins, pita bread triangles or crisp lettuce leaves

Sun-dried Tomato and Caramelised Onion Tapenade

INGREDIENTS — **Serves 4**

1 tbsp	olive oil
1 tbsp	sugar
4 cups	sliced white onions
½ cup	sun-dried tomatoes
½ tsp	salt
½ tsp	pepper
½ tsp	crushed garlic
1 tsp	mixed dried herbs
¼ cup	Vegetable Stock (page 166)

To serve

Salted crackers or toasted French bread

METHOD

Heat oil in a frying pan; add sugar and onions and cook for 15 minutes or till onions are caramelised. Add the remaining ingredients and continue cooking for 10 more minutes. Remove from heat and cool. Transfer to a blender and purée to the desired consistency. Serve with crackers or toast.

Vegetable Mould

INGREDIENTS **Serves 8-10**

2 medium	carrots, grated
½ cup	breadcrumbs

For the potato mixture

8 large	potatoes, boiled and mashed
¼ cup	sago, soaked for half an hour and drained
1 tbsp	toasted and ground peanuts
1 tbsp	ginger-chilli paste
2 tbsp	lemon juice

Salt to taste

For the green pea mixture

2 tbsp	oil
1½ cups	shelled green peas, crushed
2 tbsp	chopped fresh coriander leaves
2 tbsp	grated coconut
1 tbsp	lemon juice
1 tbsp	ginger-chilli paste
1 tsp	garam masala

A pinch of asafoetida
A pinch of soda bicarbonate
Salt to taste

To serve

Green Chutney (page 236) or tomato ketchup

METHOD

Preheat the oven to 200°C/400°F/Gas Mark 6. Spread the grated carrot at the bottom of a greased 8-inch ring mould tin. Sprinkle breadcrumbs all over.

For the potato mixture

Mix two-thirds of the mashed potato with the drained sago. Add the remaining ingredients and mix well. Press some of the mixture at the bottom and around the sides of the mould. Set aside a little mixture for the top.

For the green pea mixture

In a small saucepan, heat oil and add asafoetida. Add the peas and soda bicarbonate. Cook until soft. Remove from heat and set aside to cool. Add the remaining mashed potato, coriander leaves, grated coconut, lemon juice, ginger-chilli paste, garam masala and salt. Mix well. Layer the mixture over the potatoes. Top with a little of the reserved potato mixture. Bake in the preheated oven for 20 minutes. Remove and cool slightly. Unmould on a serving dish. Serve hot with green chutney or tomato ketchup.

Vegetable Open Sandwiches

INGREDIENTS **Serves 6-8**

200 gms	cream cheese
2/3-cup	Mayonnaise (page 230)
½ cup	chopped and boiled broccoli
½ cup	chopped and boiled cauliflower
1 small	red or yellow pepper, chopped
1 tsp	finely chopped onion
1 tsp	finely chopped garlic
1 tsp	finely chopped dried oregano
1 tsp	finely chopped basil
10-12 slices	white or brown bread

Butter to spread
Salt and pepper to taste

To garnish
Shredded cabbage and carrots

METHOD

In a medium bowl, mix together cheese, mayonnaise, broccoli, cauliflower, pepper, onion, garlic, oregano, basil, salt and pepper. Place in a refrigerator to chill.

Cut 2-inch rounds out of each bread slice. Butter lightly and cover with a damp cloth and set aside. Garnish the serving tray with shredded cabbage and carrots. Spread 1-2 tablespoons of cheese and vegetable mixture on each round and arrange on the prepared tray. Serve cold.

Vegetable Satay with Peanut Pesto

INGREDIENTS

Serves 4-6

For the vegetables

1 medium	zucchini, cut into 1/4-inch thick slices
2 small	eggplants, cut into 1/4-inch thick slices
4-6	mushroom caps, washed and halved
4-6	baby onions, peeled and blanched
4-6	broccoli or cauliflower florets
1/4 cup	peanut oil
10-12	wooden skewers

Salt and pepper to taste

For the peanut pesto

2 cups	roasted peanuts, skin removed
2 large	shallots, sliced
4 cloves	garlic
3	bird's eye chillies
3	kaffir lime leaves
2	lemon grass sticks, finely chopped
1 tbsp	sugar
1/2 cup	peanut oil
1/2 cup	basil leaves
1/4 cup	coriander leaves

Juice of 1 lemon
Salt and pepper to taste

To garnish

Roasted peanuts

METHOD

Soak wooden skewers in water. Thread one slice of each vegetable on one stick. Repeat for remaining vegetables on remaining sticks. Slightly oil and season the vegetables with salt and pepper. Grill for 4-5 minutes until tender and crisp. Keep warm.

For the peanut pesto

Process the peanuts, shallots, garlic, chillies, kaffir lime leaves and lemon grass in a blender to make a smooth purée. Add sugar, lemon juice, salt and pepper. Pour in the peanut oil and the basil and coriander leaves. Blend again until smooth. Adjust the seasoning and pour into a serving bowl. Lay a bed of peanuts on a large plate. Serve the pesto in a bowl surrounded with the vegetable satays.

Vegetable Spring Rings

INGREDIENTS — **Makes 12-15 pieces**

12-15	spring roll wrappers
2 tsp	cornflour mixed with ¼ cup water
Oil for deep-frying	

For the filling

2 tbsp	oil
1	onion, finely chopped
1	carrot, shredded
½ cup	shredded cabbage
½ cup	shredded capsicum
½ cup	bean sprouts, roughly chopped
6-8	French beans, chopped
½ tsp	pepper
½ tsp	sugar
½ tsp	MSG (optional)
½ cup	boiled noodles
1 tsp	soy sauce
Salt to taste	

To serve

Chilli sauce

METHOD

For the filling

Heat oil in a pan; fry onion and vegetables for one minute. Add salt, pepper, sugar and MSG (if using). Chop the noodles roughly and add them to the vegetable mixture along with soy sauce. Mix well. Remove from heat and set aside to cool.

For the spring rings

Cut each spring roll wrapper into squares of the required size. Place 1 tablespoon of the vegetable mixture in the centre. Brush all four sides with cornflour paste and roll the wrapper starting from one corner till the end. Lift both the ends and stick them together to form a ring. Seal the edges. When ready to serve, deep-fry the rings in hot oil until crisp. Drain on kitchen paper. Serve at once with chilli sauce.

Note: For smaller rings, cut spring roll wrappers into 2-inch squares. For larger rings, cut into 4-inch squares.

Vegetable Vadas
(Guliappa Paddu)

INGREDIENTS

Makes 14-16 pieces

2 cups	ready-mixed idli batter
¼ cup	grated carrot
¼ cup	grated cabbage
¼ cup	grated onions
2 tbsp	chopped fresh coriander
2 tbsp	chopped tomato
2 tbsp	chopped green chillies
1 tsp	fruit salt
1 tsp	salt

A pinch of asafoetida
Clarified butter

To serve

1 cup Tomato Chutney (recipe follows)

METHOD

Bring idli batter to room temperature and add all the ingredients except clarified butter. Heat a munk pan and grease each depression with a little clarified butter. Drop 1-2 tablespoons of prepared mixture in each mould, cover and cook on medium heat. Remove the lid and gently turn the vada over with the help of the stick provided with the pan. Cook again till golden brown on both sides. Serve hot with tomato chutney.

Tomato Chutney

INGREDIENTS

2 tsp	oil
1 medium	onion, finely chopped
4 medium	ripe tomatoes, quartered
1 tbsp	toasted and powdered sesame seeds
1 tbsp	toasted and powdered peanuts
2 tsp	chilli powder
1 tsp	powdered cumin seeds
1 tbsp	jaggery

Salt to taste

METHOD

Heat oil in a frying pan; fry onions till transparent. Add tomatoes and cook till they become limp and darker in colour. Add all the spice powders. Remove from heat, cool and grind with salt and jaggery to a smooth paste. Serve at room temperature.

Vegetable Wraps

INGREDIENTS

Serves 6

2 tbsp	oil
1 cup	mixed vegetables, cut into 1-inch strips (French beans, carrots, asparagus, peppers, baby corn etc.)
½ cup	yellow corn kernels, boiled
2 tbsp	finely chopped jalapeño chillies
1 tsp	taco seasoning
1 cup	grated Cheddar cheese
4	12-inch (or 8 six-inch) flour tortillas
Salt to taste	

To serve

Red Salsa (page 234)

Method

Preheat the oven to 190°C/375°F/Gas Mark 5. Heat oil in a frying pan and stir-fry the vegetables and corn over high heat till crisp and tender. Add jalapeño peppers, taco seasoning and salt. Sprinkle cheese evenly on all the tortillas. Spoon 2-3 tablespoons of the vegetable mixture on top. Roll up the tortillas tightly. Arrange on a baking sheet and bake for 10-12 minutes or till the cheese melts. Serve hot with red salsa.

Vietnamese Rolls
(Ha Gio)

INGREDIENTS **Makes 12 rolls**

1 tbsp	sesame oil
2 cloves	garlic, crushed
2-3	spring onion stems, finely chopped
1 package	bean sprouts, roughly chopped
2-3	fresh mushrooms, washed and chopped
1 medium	carrot, diced
1 tsp	soy sauce
1 tsp	chilli sauce
1 tsp	sugar
2-3 tbsp	roasted and ground peanuts
½ cup	vermicelli noodles, boiled and drained
12	rice paper sheets or wrappers

Salt and pepper to taste

For the sauce

1	chopped green chilli
1 clove	garlic, finely chopped
1 tbsp	soy sauce
1 tbsp	sugar
1 tbsp	chopped fresh coriander
1 tbsp	water
1 tsp	lemon juice

METHOD

Heat oil in a wok and stir-fry garlic, spring onions, bean sprouts, mushrooms and carrots for 2 minutes. Add soy sauce and water and cook for 3 to 4 minutes. Remove from heat and add chilli sauce, sugar, salt, pepper, peanuts and boiled vermicelli. Set aside to cool. Sprinkle both sides of the rice paper with water until soft and pliable. Place a heaped tablespoon of the stuffing in the centre. Fold the left and right sides of rice paper into the centre, and then roll up from the bottom edge to the far end. Either steam over boiling water or deep-fry. Serve with chilli sauce.

For the sauce

Mix all the ingredients in a serving bowl and set aside for thirty minutes.

Note: Steamed rolls can be stir-fried with spring onions and garlic in a little oil just before serving.

Warm Mushroom Dip

INGREDIENTS **Makes 2½ cups**

2 tbsp	butter
1 medium	onion, chopped
1 large	clove garlic, chopped
200 gms	fresh mushrooms, chopped
2 tbsp	plain flour
200 gms	cream cheese
2 tsp	Worcestershire sauce
½ cup	Sour Cream (page 234)
1 tsp	lemon juice
1 tsp	dried mixed herbs

Salt and pepper to taste

To serve

Melba toast or crackers

METHOD

In a heavy saucepan, melt butter and sauté onion, garlic and mushrooms till the liquid evaporates. Stir in the flour, salt and pepper. Add cream cheese and Worcestershire sauce and continue to cook until the cheese melts. Blend in sour cream, lemon juice and herbs. Cook until heated through. Serve warm with Melba toast or crackers.

Wonton Cups

INGREDIENTS

Serves 6

For the wonton cups

24 wonton wrappers
3-4 tbsp oil or butter to brush the wrappers

For the filling

1 tbsp oil
1 tbsp finely chopped garlic
1 tbsp finely chopped green chillies
1 tbsp red chilli paste
100 gms cabbage, finely chopped
100 gms onions, finely chopped
5-6 button mushrooms, stemmed and chopped
1 tbsp soy sauce
1 tbsp rice vinegar
½ cup noodles, boiled and chopped
Salt and pepper to taste .
A pinch of MSG (optional)

To serve

Chilli Sauce

METHOD

For the wonton cups

Trim the edges of each wrapper slightly. Use 2 wrappers at a time, and cover the rest to prevent them from drying out. Brush the wrappers lightly with oil or butter and place one on top of the other in such a way that the four corners are diagonal to each other. Press the square into a cupcake tin. Repeat for all the wrappers. Bake the wonton cups in a moderate oven for 10-15 minutes till the edges are golden brown. Remove and set aside to cool. Store in an airtight tin till ready to use.

For the filling

Heat one tablespoon of oil in a frying pan and fry the garlic, chilli and chilli paste for a few seconds. Add the vegetables, MSG (if using), soy sauce, vinegar, salt and pepper. Cook till vegetables are soft. Add the noodles and mix well. Spoon the mixture into the wonton cups and serve immediately with chilli sauce.

Mayonnaise

INGREDIENTS

Makes 1 cup

1	egg
1/2 tsp	salt
1/2 tsp	pepper
1/2 tsp	mustard
1/2 tsp	sugar
1/2-3/4 cup	salad oil
2 tbsp	vinegar or lemon juice

METHOD

Place the egg, salt, pepper, mustard and sugar in a blender and blend at medium speed. Add oil in a very thin stream, blending at high speed. DO NOT add the oil too quickly or the mayonnaise will curdle. When thick, add vinegar or lemon juice and continue blending until mixed completely. Taste and adjust the seasoning. Store in an airtight container in the refrigerator.

VARIATIONS

Garlic Mayonnaise (Aioli)

Add 2 cloves of garlic while blending the mayonnaise to make garlic mayonnaise (aioli).

Curried Mayonnaise

Add 1 teaspoon curry powder and 2 tablespoons finely chopped onion to make curried mayonnaise.

Soy Mayonnaise

Makes 1 cup

Blend together 1 cup soy milk, 4 tsp rice syrup, salt, pepper, mustard and sugar to taste. Pour into a blender jar. With the motor running, add 1 cup salad oil very slowly, until the mixture is thick. Transfer to a jar and refrigerate.

Eggless Mayonnaise

INGREDIENTS **Makes 1½ cups**

200 gms	fresh cream
2 tsp	mustard powder
½ tsp	salt
½ tsp	pepper
2 tbsp	sugar
¼ cup	salad oil
3 tsp	white vinegar or lemon juice

METHOD

In a stainless steel bowl, combine fresh cream with mustard, salt, pepper and sugar. Place over a bowl of crushed ice and beat with a beater until thick. Gradually add the oil, beating continuously, till completely absorbed in the cream. Add vinegar or lemon juice and chill until ready to serve.

Potato Mayonnaise

INGREDIENTS **Makes 1 cup**

1 small	potato, baked
1 tsp	mustard
1 tsp	salt
1 tsp	powdered sugar
2 tbsp	vinegar
¾ cup	olive oil or salad oil

METHOD

Cut the potato in half. Scoop out the insides of the potato and mash well. Add mustard, salt, and powdered sugar and 1 tbsp vinegar, and rub the mixture through a fine sieve. Beat the mixture with an electric beater or process in a blender. Slowly add the oil and remaining vinegar, blending continuously till smooth.

Marinara Sauce

INGREDIENTS **Makes 3 cups**

2 tbsp	olive oil
2 medium	onions, finely chopped
1 large	carrot, grated
1 large	green capsicum, finely chopped
4 cloves	garlic, minced
1 kg	tomatoes, blanched and chopped
1 cup	tomato purée
2 tbsp	salt
½ tbsp	pepper
1 tbsp	mixed dried herbs
1	bay leaf

METHOD

In a saucepan, heat olive oil, and sauté the onions, carrot, green capsicum and garlic. Cook until the vegetables are tender. Add the remaining ingredients and bring to a boil. Remove from heat. At this point, you could purée half the sauce and mix with the rest.

Pesto Sauce

INGREDIENTS **Makes 1 cup**

1½ cups	fresh basil leaves, stripped from their stems
1 tsp	salt
2 tsp	pepper
1 tbsp	finely chopped garlic
5 tsp	chopped and toasted walnuts or pine nuts
¾ cup	olive oil
50 gms	freshly grated Parmesan cheese.

METHOD

In a blender, combine basil, salt, pepper, garlic, walnuts and oil. Blend at high speed until smooth. The sauce should be thin enough to run off a spatula easily. Transfer the sauce to a bowl and stir in the grated Parmesan cheese.

Hummus

INGREDIENTS **Makes 3 cups**

250 gms	chickpeas
3-4 tbsp	tahina paste
3-4 tbsp	lemon juice
6-8 cloves	garlic
1 tbsp	finely chopped parsley
1 tbsp	finely chopped basil (optional)

A pinch of soda
Salt to taste

To garnish
Olive oil and chilli powder

METHOD

Soak the chickpeas in water for 6 hours with a pinch of soda. Cook in a pressure cooker until very soft. Drain and set aside to cool. Reserve the water from the cooker. Place the chickpeas in a food processor with tahina paste, salt, lemon juice, garlic, parsley and basil. Process till you get a thick paste. Add about 3-4 tablespoons of reserved water from the cooker if the mixture is too dry. Transfer the ground paste to a serving bowl and adjust the salt and lemon juice.

Sour Cream

INGREDIENTS — **Makes 1½ cups**

1 cup	thick yogurt
100 gms	fresh cream, whipped
1 tbsp	white vinegar or lemon juice
Salt to taste	

METHOD

Sieve yogurt to make it smooth and creamy. Fold in the whipped cream along with vinegar and salt. Mix well. Chill for 1 hour before serving.

Red Salsa

INGREDIENTS — **Makes ½ a cup**

4	tomatoes, cut into large pieces
1	onion, cut into large pieces
5-6 cloves	garlic
4	Kashmiri chillies
1 tbsp	chopped coriander leaves
2 tbsp	chopped jalapeño chillies
1 tbsp	vinegar
1 tsp	taco seasoning
A large pinch of oregano	
Salt to taste	

METHOD

Process all the ingredients in a blender or a food processor to make a chunky mixture. Do not make a fine purée.

Refried Beans

INGREDIENTS **Makes 3 cups**

200 gms	kidney beans
1	onion, roughly chopped
2-3 cloves	garlic
1 tbsp	taco seasoning
2 tbsp	Red Salsa (page 234)

Salt to taste

METHOD

Soak the beans overnight or for 6-8 hours. Place in a pressure cooker with onion, garlic and salt. Cook till the pressure is released 3-4 times (3-4 whistles). Remove from heat and set aside to cool. Remove from pressure cooker and mash lightly; add taco seasoning and salsa.

Chutneys

Coconut Chutney **Makes 1½ cups**

Mix together 1 cup grated coconut, 1 chopped green chilli, 1 inch ginger, 1 tbsp chopped coriander leaves, 1 tbsp sugar and 1 tbsp soaked split Bengal gram. Grind the mixture and stir in half a cup of thick yogurt and salt to taste.

Mint Chutney **Makes 1 cup**

In a small blender jar, mix together 1 cup mint leaves, ½ cup coriander leaves, juice of 1 lemon, 1 tsp ginger-chilli paste, 1 tbsp grated coconut, 1 clove garlic (optional), salt and sugar to taste and a little cold water. Blend to make a smooth paste. Refrigerate until ready to use.

Green Chutney **Makes 1 cup**

In a small blender jar, mix together ½ cup fresh coriander leaves, ½ cup mint leaves, 3 tbsp grated coconut, 4 green chillies, ½ inch ginger, juice of 1 lemon, salt and sugar to taste. Blend to make a smooth paste.

Garlic Chutney **Makes 1/2 cup**

Soak 50 dried red chillies for 15 minutes in water. Pound ½ cup of garlic cloves with a mortar and pestle. Add 3 teaspoons salt and 1 teaspoon cumin seeds. Make a paste with a little oil.

Sweet and Sour Chutney **Makes 1½ half cups**

Cook 200 gms of dates and a walnut-sized ball of tamarind, 2 cups of water, salt, black salt and chilli powder to taste in a pressure cooker for 2-3 whistles. Cool. Blend in a liquidiser jar and strain. If the chutney is to thin, cook for 5-10 minuts till thick.

Mocktails

They are smooth, they are colourful, they perk you up…but they are not alcoholic! Welcome to the world of mocktails or 'mock cocktails'. A unique blend of fresh fruit juices, syrups, cream, herbs, spices, and sometimes a dash of fizz, mocktails look great and taste even better.

Glassware

Shot glass
60 ml

Old-Fashioned/
Rocks/Whiskey
230 ml

Highball
280 ml

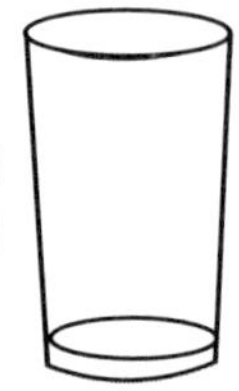

Pilsner
280 ml

Collins
340 ml

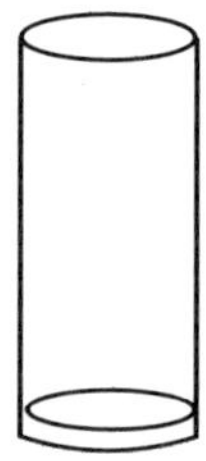

Cordial or liqueur
60 ml

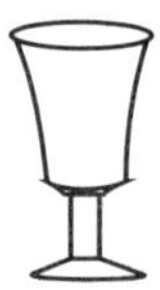

Margarita/
Champagne
Saucer
140 ml

Fluted Champagne
140 ml

Cocktail
140 ml

Wine
200 ml

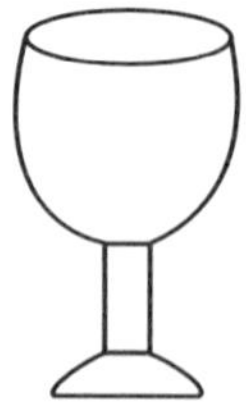

Snifter/
Brandy Balloon
310 ml

Goblet
340 ml

Pina Colada
400 ml

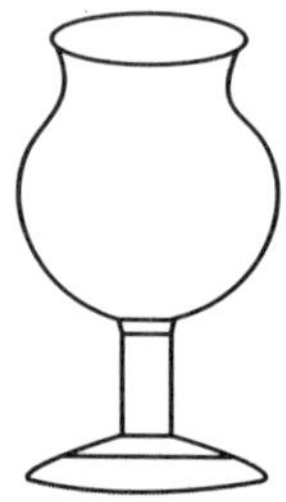

Angel's Punch

INGREDIENTS **Serves 10-12**

4 cups	white grape juice
¼ cup	lemon juice
½ cup	sugar syrup
1 tbsp	ginger juice
2 cups	green tea
7-inch round	block of ice
500 ml	club soda

To garnish
Fresh mint leaves and thinly sliced lemon

METHOD

Mix together all the ingredients, except club soda, and place in a refrigerator until well chilled. Pour the chilled mixture into a punch bowl and add the block of ice. Add soda and stir gently. Garnish with mint leaves and lemon slices and serve in stemmed glasses.

Note: This drink is poured into a bowl, so that guests can help themselves to the drink.

Vegetable Medley

INGREDIENTS **Serves 2**

1	spring onion stem
2 medium	carrots
2 medium	tomatoes
1 stick	celery
½ medium	cucumber
½ medium	red pepper
2-3	basil leaves
2-3 drops	Tabasco
1 tsp	lemon juice
Salt to taste	
Ice cubes	

METHOD

Wash and chop all the vegetables into bite-size pieces. Put them all into a juicer or blender and process till smooth. Remove into a tall container, add crushed ice and blend with a hand mixer. Serve chilled.

Watermelon Refresher

INGREDIENTS **Serves 8-10**

6 cups	watermelon pieces, deseeded
1½ cups	orange juice
1½ cups	lemonade
Crushed ice	

To garnish

A few mint leaves and a wedge of watermelon

METHOD

In a liquidiser, blend together watermelon, orange juice and half cup of crushed ice till smooth. Pour into a jug and top up with lemonade. Add more ice if required. Garnish with mint leaves and watermelon and serve in tall glasses.

Apple Tang Fizz

INGREDIENTS **Serves 2**

2 tbsp	orange Tang powder
1 glass	apple juice
2 tsp	lemon juice
4-6 cubes	ice
Soda water	

To garnish

A few apple pieces and mint leaves

METHOD

Place ice cubes, Tang powder in 2 high ball glasses. Divide the apple and lemon juice between the two glasses. Stir well till all the powder is mixed. Top up with soda. Garnish with apple pieces and mint leaves and serve at once.

Apple-Cinnamon Drink

INGREDIENTS **Serves 6-8**

2 medium	oranges
14-16	cloves
½ cup	rock sugar
2 sticks	cinnamon
2 litres	apple juice

METHOD

Stud the oranges with cloves. Mix sugar and ½ cup water together in a saucepan and heat gently. When the sugar has melted, add the clove studded-oranges, cinnamon stick and apple juice. Simmer over a low heat for half an hour. Serve hot or cold. To serve cold, drain the spices and top with crushed ice. Serve in a cup.

Coral Punch

INGREDIENTS **Serves 20**

3 cups	pineapple juice
3 cups	orange juice
2 cups	cranberry juice
1 cup	apple juice
500 ml	ginger ale
4 cups	lemonade
Ice cubes	

To garnish
Mint leaves

METHOD

In a punch bowl, mix all the juices together and top up with ice, ginger ale and lemonade. Garnish with mint leaves. Pour into stemmed glasses and serve.

Cranberry Cooler

INGREDIENTS **Serves 12**

4 cups	cranberry juice
1 cup	white grape juice
200 ml	lemonade
200 ml	soda water
Crushed ice	

To garnish
Assorted chopped fruit and mint leaves

METHOD

Chill all the ingredients separately. Just before serving, mix in a punch bowl and garnish with fruit and mint leaves.

Apple Pie Shake

INGREDIENTS **Serves 2**

½ cup	brown sugar
1	2-inch cinnamon, crushed
2 cups	apple juice or
3 cups	sliced apples, puréed
½ teaspoon	lemon juice
1 scoop	vanilla ice cream
Crushed ice	

To garnish

Finely chopped apples, powdered cinnamon, crushed butter cookies and a piece of candy

METHOD

Heat sugar, half cup water and cinnamon stick together in a small saucepan until sugar melts and attains a syrupy consistency. Strain and set aside to cool. In a blender, process together the apple juice, lemon juice, sugar syrup and vanilla ice cream until frothy. If the consistency is too thick, add some crushed ice. Blend until smooth. Pour into tall glasses. Sprinkle apple pieces, cinnamon powder and crushed butter cookies on top and stick a candy on the edge. Serve immediately.

Fruit Juice Cooler

INGREDIENTS **Serves 4**

½ cup grape juice
1¼ cups peach juice
½ cup orange juice
2 tbsp lemon juice
1¼ cups soda water or water
Ice

To garnish
Assorted chopped fruit

METHOD

Mix together all the fruit juices and chill. Just before serving, place the juice mixture in a blender jar with ice cubes and blend until frothy. Pour into glasses till two-third full. Top up with soda and garnish with chopped fruit.

Fruit Punch

INGREDIENTS **Serves 8**

1 cup sugar
2 cups orange juice
¼ cup lemon juice
2 tbsp ginger juice
2 cups black tea, cooled
2 bottles (200 ml each) soda water
Crushed ice

To garnish
A few lemon slices and fresh mint leaves

METHOD

Combine 1 cup water and sugar to make a syrup. Heat till sugar dissolves. Cool. Combine all the juices with sugar syrup and tea. Chill. Take a tall glass, pour the juice mixture until the glass is three-fourth full. Top with chilled soda and crushed ice. Garnish with lemon slices and mint leaves.

Fruit Salad Smoothie

INGREDIENTS **Serves 2**

1 cup	chopped mixed fruit (banana, strawberries, apple, orange)
2 scoops	vanilla ice cream
3-4	ice cubes
2 tbsp	honey

METHOD

Place all the ingredients in a blender and blend until smooth. Pour into tall glasses and serve.

Golden Ambrosia

INGREDIENTS **Serves 12-15**

1 cup	sugar
1 litre	orange juice
750 ml	pineapple juice
1 litre	ginger ale (such as Canada Dry), chilled
2	oranges, segmented

To garnish
Mint leaves and lemon slices

METHOD

Combine the sugar and 3 cups water in a pan. Stir over low heat until the sugar has dissolved. Mix together both the juices and chill in a refrigerator. Just before serving, add the chilled ginger ale and orange segments. Decorate with fresh mint leaves and lemon slices.

Note: For an alcoholic cocktail, take one large peg (60 ml) of vodka, one small peg (30 ml) of peach schnapps and pour the prepared mixture into the glass.

Grapefruit Cocktail

INGREDIENTS **Serves 2**

1½ cups	grapefruit juice
1 cup	orange juice
200 ml	soda water

A splash of grenadine
Ice

To garnish
A few mint leaves and slices of orange

METHOD

Mix both the juices in a jug filled with ice. Pour in the soda to fizz it up and add a splash of grenadine. Pour into highball glasses and serve at once, garnished with mint and slices of orange.

Kahwa

INGREDIENTS **Serves 4**

4 level tsp	green tea leaves
¼ tsp	saffron threads, powdered
2	cardamoms, crushed
1	½-inch cinnamon, crushed
2	cloves, crushed
8	almonds, blanched and chopped

Sugar to taste

METHOD

Place tea leaves in a saucepan and pour 600 ml boiling water over them. Allow to infuse over a very low heat. Dissolve saffron in a little water by rubbing the threads gently. Strain the tea into another saucepan and add the saffron along with all the other ingredients. Serve hot.

Land's End Sunset

INGREDIENTS **Serves 2**

2 medium	peaches or apricots, peeled and stoned
300 ml	pineapple juice

Crushed ice
Lemonade or Sprite
A dash of grenadine

To garnish
Sliced orange

METHOD

Blend peaches or apricots with pineapple juice and crushed ice in a blender until smooth. Pour into Pilsner glasses. Top with Sprite or lemonade. Add a few drops of grenadine but do not stir the drink. Garnish with orange slices and serve.

Lemon and Lime Cooler

INGREDIENTS **Serves 2**

3 tbsp	sugar
1 glass (200 ml)	sweet lime juice

Juice of ½ a lemon
A dash of Campari
Crushed ice

To garnish
Lemon slices and mint leaves

METHOD

Stir the lemon juice and sugar until the sugar dissolves. Mix together with the sweet lime juice. Place crushed ice at the bottom of 2 glasses, pour the lemon juices over and gently drizzle the Campari over the mixture. Do not stir. Garnish each glass with a slice of lemon and mint leaves and serve.

Berry Tang

INGREDIENTS **Serves 1**

¼ cup cranberry, blackberry or strawberry juice
1 tbsp lemon juice
Ice cubes
200 ml tonic water

To garnish
Slice of lemon

METHOD

Mix the juices together in a tall glass. Add 4-5 ice cubes and top up with tonic water. Garnish and serve immediately.

Blue Hawaii

INGREDIENTS **Serves 1**

3 tbsp blue curaçao syrup
3 tbsp Sweet and Sour Mix (page 277)
100 ml club soda
Splashes of orange juice and pineapple juice
Crushed ice

To garnish
Pineapple slice, orange slice and lemon slice

METHOD

In a highball glass, place half cup crushed ice, blue curaçao syrup and sweet and sour mix. Top with soda and splashes of both the juices. Garnish with fruit slices and serve.

Candy Bar Smoothie

INGREDIENTS **Serves 4**

2 candy bars of your choice (Kit Kat, Twix, Mars etc.)
1 cup vanilla ice cream
1 cup sweetened condensed milk
½ cup grated milk chocolate
2 cups crushed ice

To garnish
Whipped cream

METHOD

Combine all the ingredients in a blender. Blend until smooth. Pour into tall glasses, garnish with whipped cream and serve.

Carnival Punch

INGREDIENTS **Serves 10**

4 cups unsweetened orange juice
2 cups grapefruit juice
1 cup white grape juice
1 cup apple juice
15 ice cubes
1 cup mixed black and white grapes, washed and halved
A few sprigs of mint

METHOD

Place the ice cubes in a large punch bowl or jug. Add all the other ingredients and mix well. Chill for at least 15 minutes before serving.

Variation: To make an alcoholic version of this drink, add 1 peg (30 ml) of vodka or white rum per serving.

Cherry Lemonade

INGREDIENTS **Serves 8**

½ cup sugar
¼ cup lemon juice
500 gms fresh cherries, stemmed, pitted and washed
500 ml soda water
Crushed ice

To garnish
Mint leaves

METHOD

Place the sugar, lemon juice and ¼ cup water in a saucepan and heat gently until the sugar melts. Add the cherries and cook until they are slightly wilted. Remove from heat and pass through a sieve. Set aside to cool. Pour half a cup of cherry mixture into each glass and top with crushed ice and soda. Garnish with mint leaves and serve.

Coconut Refresher

INGREDIENTS **Serves 4**

2 tender coconuts
2 tsps sugar
½ tsp lemon juice
½ cup finely diced apple
A small pinch of salt
Splashes of grenadine

To garnish
A few red rose petals

METHOD

Chill the coconuts in their shells thoroughly. Remove water and the flesh. Blend both together with sugar and lemon juice in a liquidiser till smooth. Add a pinch of salt. Pour into glasses and add apple pieces and splashes of grenadine. Decorate with rose petals and serve.

Lemon Snow Mist

INGREDIENTS **Serves 4**

1 cup whipping cream
500 ml Sprite or lemonade

For lemon curd

4 tbsp lemon juice
1½ cups cold milk
¾ cup sugar
4 tbsp cornflour
1 tbsp butter

METHOD

For the lemon curd, mix all the ingredients in a saucepan and heat gently, stirring continuously. Remove from heat when the mixture is thick and transparent. Set aside to cool. Whip the cream until it forms soft peaks. Fold it into the lemon curd when it is completely cold. Mix well. Freeze the mixture for 3-4 hours or overnight. Put a scoop of frozen lemon cream into a tall pilsner glass. Top up with chilled Sprite. Add the Sprite gently to prevent the froth from overflowing. Serve with a straw.

Mint and Lemon Iced Tea

INGREDIENTS **Serves 16**

8 tea bags
Sugar cubes
Juice of 4 lemons
Ice cubes
A fistful of mint leaves

METHOD

Combine the tea bags and 4 cups water in a glass jug. Set aside for 1-6 hours. Remove the tea bags. Add sugar and lemon juice and top up with ice cubes and mint. Serve chilled.

Pineapple Crush

INGREDIENTS **Serves 10**

2½ cups	unsweetened pineapple juice
1 litre	ginger ale (such as Canada Dry)

Juice of 1 orange
Juice of 1 lemon
Sugar to taste
Ice cubes

For the pineapple sorbet cubes

2 tsp	unflavoured gelatine
6 tbsp	sugar
3 tbsp	lemon juice
1¼ cups	pineapple juice

A few pieces of mixed chopped fruit
Pinch of salt

METHOD

Combine the fruit juices in a large punch bowl and sweeten to taste. Chill well in a refrigerator.

For the pineapple sorbet cubes
Mix together the gelatine, sugar and 150 ml water in a pan. Soak for a few minutes. Place the pan on heat and stir until the sugar and gelatine dissolve. Cool and strain. Mix the lemon juice, pineapple juice and salt. Pour this mixture into an ice tray. Arrange the chopped fruit in each cube and freeze until set. When ready to serve, add the ginger ale and sorbet cubes to the punch bowl. Serve at once.

Mock Champagne

INGREDIENTS **Serves 12**

2/3 cup sugar
1 cup grapefruit juice
½ cup orange juice
800 ml lemonade or ginger ale
3 tbsp grenadine
Crushed ice

To garnish
Orange slices, and glace cherries

METHOD

Mix sugar and two-third cup water in a saucepan and simmer over a medium heat for 10 minutes. Cool. Add the syrup to both the juices in a jug. Chill thoroughly. Just before serving, add lemonade or ginger ale, grenadine and crushed ice. Pour into champagne glasses and garnish with orange segments and glacé cherries.

Mock Sangria

INGREDIENTS **Serves 12**

½ cup rock sugar
1 1-inch cinnamon
½ cup bite-sized pieces of pineapple
1 large orange, sliced
750 ml red or white grape juice
500 ml soda water
10-12 ice cubes

METHOD

Make a syrup with rock sugar, water and the cinnamon. Soak the chopped fruit in warm syrup for half an hour. Chill the juice and soda separately. Half an hour before serving, pour the sugar syrup with the fruit into a large jug. Add the juice and soda and top up with ice cubes. Serve in stemmed glasses.

Orange and Pineapple Fizz

INGREDIENTS **Serves 6**

1 packet	orange jelly crystals
1 large	fresh pineapple, peeled and chopped
2 tbsp	lemon juice
1 cup	orange juice
500 ml	Sprite or lemonade

A few ice cubes

To garnish
Mint leaves, lemon and orange slices
Grenadine

METHOD

Mix together the orange juice and jelly crystals in a saucepan and heat gently until dissolved. Set aside to cool. Place chopped pineapple and lemon juice in a liquidiser jar and blend until smooth. With the motor running, add the cooled jelly mixture in a thin stream. Add ice cubes and continue blending until the liquid is frothy. Pour into a jug or a punch bowl and add Sprite or lemonade. Garnish with mint leaves, lemon and orange slices. Very gently, drizzle grenadine, over the mixture. Serve in stemmed or Collins glasses with paper umbrellas.

Note: Use 30 ml Bacardi rum per glass for an alcoholic version.

Orange and Strawberry Julius

INGREDIENTS — **Serves 4**

¾ cup	orange juice, chilled
¾ cup	strawberry juice, chilled
1 cup	cold milk
3-4 tbsp	sugar
5-6	ice cubes
½ teaspoon	vanilla essence

METHOD

Place all the ingredients in a liquidiser jar and blend until frothy. Pour into glasses and serve right away.

Note: This is an excellent breakfast drink.

Mango Squash

INGREDIENTS — **Makes 20 glasses**

1 litre	Alphonso mango juice, sieved (approx. 10 mangoes)
1 kg (approx)	sugar
2 tbsp	citric acid
½ tsp	sodium benzoate
½ tsp	potassium meta bi sulphate (optional)

METHOD

Measure the juice with a cup measure. Take an equal quantity of sugar and mix with 1 litre water and bring to a boil. Add citric acid when the sugar has completely melted. Boil it for 3-4 minutes further and remove from stove. Strain the sugar syrup and set aside to cool. Add sieved mango pulp to the syrup and mix well. If you are using a preservative, mix the powder in a little of the juice and add it to the mixture. Fill in glass bottles and store in the refrigerator. Use 3-4 tablespoons of this squash mixed with three-fourth glass of cold water and ice to get 1 glass of mango squash.

Note: To get a smooth drink, mix the squash and water with rod blender before adding the ice.

Oreo Cookie Milkshake

INGREDIENTS **Serves 1**

3	Oreo cookies
1 cup	cold milk
1 scoop	vanilla ice cream
2-3 drops	vanilla essence
Sugar to taste	
2-3	ice cubes

To garnish
Whipped cream

METHOD

Crush the cookies and set a few pieces aside for garnishing. Put the remaining ingredients into a blender and process till well blended. Pour into a tall glass and garnish with whipped cream. Serve immediately.

Party Fizz

INGREDIENTS **Serves 12**

4	lemons, thinly sliced
3 medium	oranges, thinly sliced
2 tbsp	fine sugar
1 litre	ginger ale (such as Canada Dry)
500 ml	soda water
100 gms	crystallised ginger
15	ice cubes

METHOD

Place the fruit slices in a punch bowl and sprinkle the sugar over. Chill for 1 hour. Just before serving, add all the other ingredients to the bowl and stir until well-blended. Serve immediately.

Peach Iced Tea

INGREDIENTS **Serves 4**

3	tea bags
3½ cups	peach juice
¼ cup	sugar syrup (recipe follows)

For the sugar syrup

11/3 cups	sugar
1¼ cups	water
2 inches	cinnamon

To garnish

Peach slices and basil sprigs

METHOD

Place tea bags in a 5-cup capacity heatproof jug. In a saucepan, bring 4 cups water to a boil and pour over the tea bags. Allow tea to steep for 7 minutes. Pour the tea into another jug. Cover and chill for about an hour. Stir in the peach juice and syrup. Serve tea over ice in tall glasses and garnish with peach slices and basil sprigs.

For the sugar syrup

In a saucepan, bring sugar, cinnamon and water to a boil, stirring continuously until the sugar has completely dissolved. Allow the syrup to cool. Fill in a bottle and store in the refrigerator up to 2 weeks.

Sea Breeze

INGREDIENTS **Serves 20**

1 litre	pink grapefruit juice
1 litre	Lemonade
600 ml	cranberry juice
Slices of lemon	
Ice cubes	

METHOD

Chill all the ingredients separately. Just before serving, mix them and pour into tall glasses. Garnish each glass with a lemon slice and ice.

Sangrita

INGREDIENTS

Serves 6

2-3 medium	cucumbers of ½-inch diameter
2 cups	fresh tomato juice
1 cup	orange juice
2 tbsp	lemon juice
1 tbsp	minced onion
½ tsp	Worcestershire sauce
½	roasted red chilli
½ tsp	sugar

Salt, pepper and Tabasco to taste

To garnish

Freshly chopped mint

METHOD

Cut two 3½-inch lengths from each of the cucumbers to use as cups. Peel the cucumber leaving 1½-inch band of the peel at one end. Using a melon baller, scoop out the seeds stopping just before reaching the bottom. Refrigerate the cups for at least 10 minutes.

In a blender, combine the tomato, orange and lemon juices with onion and Worcestershire sauce. Crumble in roasted chilli and purée. Strain through a coarse sieve. Season sangrita with salt, pepper, sugar and Tabasco to taste. Chill for 20 minutes. Pour sangrita into the cucumber cups and serve.

Note: Sangrita is often used as a cocktail mixer or drunk alongside a shot of Tequila as a chaser. The tequila and sangrita are poured into separate shot glasses and the two are alternately sipped slowly, first the tequila and then the chilled sangrita.

Sangrita

Pomegranate Caipiroshka

Watermelon Refresher

Lemon Fizz

INGREDIENTS **Serves 2**

2 cups apple juice
2-3 tbsp lemon juice
Rind of 1 lemon
Ice cubes
Soda water

To garnish
Lemon slices, mint leaves and apple pieces

METHOD

Mix the apple and lemon juices and lemon rind in a pitcher with ice cubes. Top up with soda. Garnish with lemon slices, mint leaves and apple pieces. Pour into tall glasses and serve.

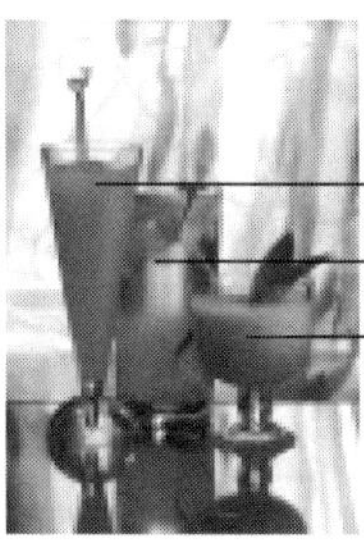

Pomegranate Caipiroshka

INGREDIENTS **Serves 1**

1 large lemon, cut into 8 pieces
6-8 fresh mint leaves
1-2 tbsp powdered sugar
2 tbsp fresh pomegranate kernels
¼ cup pomegranate juice
60 ml vodka (optional)
Crushed ice

To garnish
A dash of grenadine and wedge of lemon

METHOD

Place the lemon, mint leaves, sugar and pomegranate kernels in a stainless steel jug. Crush with a wooden pestle until partially crushed. Add the pomegranate juice and transfer the mixture to an old-fashioned glass. Add the vodka if using and fill up with crushed ice. Garnish with grenadine and a wedge of lemon.

Pomegranate Lemonade

INGREDIENTS **Serves 3**

1 litre pomegranate juice
8-10 tbsp powdered sugar
500 ml club soda
Juice of 3 lemons
A few mint leaves

METHOD

Pour pomegranate juice into ice cube trays and freeze overnight. Mix lemon juice and sugar in a bowl until sugar has dissolved. Divide the mixture among 3 tall glasses. Add 5-6 pomegranate juice ice cubes to each glass. Top up with club soda and garnish with mint leaves. Serve at once.

Pineapple Cooler

INGREDIENTS **Serves 4-6**

2 cups	fresh pineapple juice, chilled
$1\frac{1}{2}$ cups	guava juice, chilled
1 tsp	lemon juice

Sugar to taste
Crushed ice
A few drops of grenadine

To garnish
Mint leaves and pineapple pieces

METHOD
Pour all the juices and sugar to the taste into a liquidiser jar and blend at high speed for 1 minute. Transfer to a jug. Arrange stemmed glasses on a tray and spoon crushed ice into each one. Pour the juice into each glass. Swirl a few drops of grenadine into the mixture and serve immediately garnished with mint leaves and pineapple pieces.

Pineapple, Lychee and Mint Daiquiri

INGREDIENTS **Serves 4**

2 cups	fresh pineapple, diced
1 cup	lychee juice or 5-6 fresh lychees
$\frac{1}{4}$ cup	sugar
$\frac{1}{4}$ cup	lemon juice
10-12	mint leaves
2-3 cups	crushed ice

To garnish
Pineapple leaves

METHOD
Place all the ingredients in a liquidiser jar. Blend until the mixture has the consistency of shaved ice. Pour into cocktail glasses and garnish with pineapple leaves.

Sparkling Grape Juice Punch

INGREDIENTS **Serves 20**

¾ cup	sugar
2	2-inch cinnamon sticks
4 cups	red grape juice
1 tbsp	lemon juice
1 cup	orange juice
500 ml	Sprite or lemonade
500 ml	soda water
Ice cubes	

To garnish

Cinnamon, orange and lemon slices.

METHOD

In a medium-sized saucepan, combine 3 cups water, sugar and cinnamon sticks. Bring to a boil and simmer for 5 minutes. Remove from heat and chill in a refrigerator. Pour the cinnamon syrup into a punch bowl and add the remaining ingredients. Garnish with the cinnamon, orange and lemon slices and serve chilled in stemmed glasses.

Spiced Orange Tea Cooler

INGREDIENTS **Serves 6**

2 large	oranges
¼ cup	orange rind + tea leaves or
3	tea bags + 2 tsp grated orange rind
3-4 one inch	pieces ginger, sliced
1½ cups	orange juice
6-7 tbsp	rock sugar (dissolved in ½ cup of warm water and cooled)
Ice cubes	

To garnish

Mint leaves and orange slices

METHOD

Grate the rind from the whole oranges and mix them together with tea leaves. Boil 4 cups the water and pour over the tea leaves and orange rind in a teapot. Cover for 5-7 minutes. Strain and add chopped ginger to the tea and leave to cool. Add the orange juice and sugar water. Stir until the sugar dissolves. Pour the tea over ice filled in 6 glasses and garnish with mint leaves and orange slices.

Springtime Splash

INGREDIENTS **Serves 4**

2 cups	green grapes, stemmed and washed
16 medium	strawberries, hulled and washed
1 tbsp	lemon juice
1 tbsp	ginger juice (optional)
6-8	ice cubes

Sugar to taste

To garnish

Orange segments, grapes and sliced lemon

METHOD

Place grapes and strawberries in a liquidiser jar along with the ice, lemon and ginger juices. Blend until smooth. Taste and add sugar if required. Pour into tall glasses and garnish with fruit and mint. Serve immediately.

Strawberry Cheesecake Shake

INGREDIENTS **Serves 2**

2 cups	sliced fresh strawberries
½ cup	cream cheese
¼ cup	chilled milk
3 tbsp	powdered sugar
2 cups	fresh strawberry ice cream, slightly softened

To sprinkle

Sweet cookie crumbs

To garnish

Sliced strawberries

METHOD

Chill all the ingredients in the refrigerator. Place the first 4 ingredients in the blender and blend until smooth. Add ice cream and blend again. Pour into stemmed glasses and sprinkle cookie crumbs on top. Garnish with sliced strawberry and serve.

Strawberry-Kiwi Sangria

INGREDIENTS **Serves 6-8**

4	strawberry flavoured teabags
1 cup	sugar
3	kiwi fruit, peeled and cubed
750 ml	apple juice
6-8	dried rose petals or ½ teaspoon rose water
2 cups	strawberry juice
2 cups	ice cubes

METHOD

Bring 2 cups of water to a boil and add the teabags. Remove from heat, cover and set aside for 10 minutes. Discard teabags and add the sugar and another 2 cups of water to the hot tea. Refrigerate for 2-3 hours. Place the chopped fruit in a large pitcher and pour the tea over. Add the remaining ingredients. Stir and serve in stemmed glasses.

Sunrise Fruit Medley

INGREDIENTS **Serves 4**

1 cup	orange juice
1 tsp	lemon juice
1 tsp	orange Tang powder
200 ml	Sprite, chilled
Ice cubes	

To garnish

Small pieces of apple and kiwi

METHOD

Mix together the orange and lemon juices and Tang powder and chill in a refrigerator. When ready to serve, place 2-3 ice cubes in each glass and divide the juice mixture amongst them equally. Top up with Sprite and garnish with the chopped fruit.

Sunset Cooler

INGREDIENTS **Serves 2**

1 cup pomegranate juice
½ cup orange juice, with segments
1 tsp lemon juice
Ginger ale
Crushed ice

To garnish
Mint leaves

METHOD

Blend the pomegranate, orange and lemon juices with ice until smooth. Pour into tall glasses and top up with ginger ale. Garnish with mint and serve.

Tomato and Herb Drink

INGREDIENTS **Serves 2**

2 cups tomato juice
1 medium onion, grated
1 medium carrot, grated
2 celery sticks, chopped
4-5 basil leaves
½ tsp dried oregano
A dash of Tabasco
Salt and pepper to taste
A few ice cubes

To garnish
Sliced lemon and celery sticks.

METHOD

In a medium-sized saucepan, mix together tomato juice, onion, carrot and celery. Bring to a boil and remove from heat. Cool. Add the remaining ingredients and pour into tall glasses. Garnish with lemon slices and celery sticks.

Transfusion

INGREDIENTS **Serves 1**

½ cup green grape juice
3-4 drops lemon juice
1 cup ginger ale
A dash of grenadine
Ice cubes

To garnish
Lemon wedge and mint leaves

METHOD

Pour grape juice and lemon juice into a tall glass with 3-4 cubes of ice. Top with ginger ale and a dash of grenadine. Garnish with a lemon wedge and mint leaves and serve.

Tropical Punch Colada

INGREDIENTS **Serves 2**

1 cup pineapple juice
½ cup guava juice
½ cup coconut cream
½ cup white rum (optional)
2 cups ice cubes

To garnish
Mint leaves

METHOD

Chill all the ingredients separately. Pour both the juices and coconut cream into a pitcher along with the rum, if using. Fill 2 tall glasses with ice cubes and pour the drink over. Garnish with mint and serve.

Cocktails

What is a party without some high spirits to make it swing? Cocktails add zest and zing to a party, especially if you don't pull any Punches!

TIPS FOR SERVING COCKTAILS

Make a list of all the equipment required for your party and keep it ready. You should have on hand:

- Alcoholic beverages: whiskey, vodka, gin, dark and light rums, tequila, fruit liqueurs, white and red wines, beer, brandy etc.
- Non-alcoholic beverages: club soda, cola, 7-up or lemonade, tonic water, ginger ale, tomato juice, orange juice, lemon juice, grape fruit juice etc.
- Garnishes: cherries, orange and lemon wedges or slices, olives, pineapples.
- Accessories: toothpicks, swizzle sticks, cocktail napkins, jigger (30 ml and 60 ml measuring tool), cocktail shaker, ice (approximately 500 grams per head).

Some Facts About...

WHISKEY: Made from grain, corn, wheat, rye and barley

VODKA : Made from fermented mash of grains and natural spirits

GIN: Made from fermented mash of grain flavoured with juniper

BRANDY: Distilled from fermented juice and mash of fruits

WINE: Fermented mash of gold and red grapes. White wine is always served chilled and red wine is always served at room temperature.

Alabama Slammer

INGREDIENTS **Serves 1**

30 ml Southern Comfort
30 ml amaretto
15 ml sloe gin
A dash of lemon juice
Ice cubes

METHOD

Pour all the ingredients, except the lemon juice, over ice in a highball glass. Stir, add the lemon juice and serve.

Angel's Tip

INGREDIENTS **Serves 1**

20 ml brown crème de cacao
10 ml cream

To garnish

A cherry

METHOD

Pour the crème de cacao into a liqueur/cordial glass. Float the cream on top. Garnish with the cherry and serve.

Bailey's Fizz

INGREDIENTS **Serves 1**

30 ml Bailey's Irish Cream
Soda water
Ice

METHOD

Fill a highball glass with ice. Pour in the Irish cream, fill with soda and serve.

Between the Sheets

INGREDIENTS **Serves 1**

30 ml brandy
30 ml triple sec
30 ml light rum (such as Bacardi)
Ice cubes

METHOD

Mix the ingredients in a cocktail shaker with ice. Shake well and pour into a cocktail glass.

Black Velvet

INGREDIENTS **Serves 1**

300 ml chilled beer
30 ml dark rum

METHOD

Pour the rum into a beer mug. Pour the chilled beer over and serve.

Bloody Mary

INGREDIENTS **Serves 1**

30 ml
Bloody Mary Mix (recipe follows)
Ice cubes

To garnish
Celery stick and a slice of lime

METHOD

Fill a Collins glass with ice. Pour in the vodka and top with the Bloody Mary mix. Garnish with the celery stick and a slice of lime and serve.

Bloody Mary Mix
Mix together 1 litre tomato juice, 1 tsp salt, 1 tsp celery salt, 1 tsp pepper, 2 tsp grated horseradish, 120 ml Worcestershire sauce and 4 dashes of Tabasco sauce.

Blue Hawaiian

INGREDIENTS **Serves 1**

30 ml light rum
15 ml blue curaçao
Pineapple juice, as required
Ice

To garnish
Pineapple and lemon wedges

METHOD

Fill a highball glass with ice. Pour in the rum and blue curaçao and fill with pineapple juice. Garnish with the pineapple and lemon wedges and serve.

Bull Dog

INGREDIENTS **Serves 1**

45 ml gin
3-4 ice cubes
Ginger ale or soda water as required
A splash of orange juice

METHOD

Pour the gin into a highball glass with 3-4 ice cubes. Fill the glass with ginger ale or soda water. Add a splash of orange juice and serve.

Crème De Menthe Frappé

INGREDIENTS **Serves 1**

45 ml	crème de menthe
45 ml	Cointreau

Crushed ice

To garnish
A slice of lemon

METHOD

Mix the ingredients in a cocktail glass. Serve with a slice of lemon.

French 75

INGREDIENTS **Serves 1**

30 ml	gin
60 ml	Sweet and Sour Mix (recipe follows)

Champagne, as required
Ice cubes

METHOD

Fill a Collins glass with ice. Pour in the gin and sweet and sour mix. Stir well. Fill the glass with champagne and stir lightly.

Sweet and Sour Mix
Mix together half cup sugar and one-fourth cup lemon juice. Cook until sugar melts. Refrigerate till ready to use.

Banana Daiquiri

INGREDIENTS **Serves 1**

30 ml	light rum
45 ml	Sweet and Sour Mix (page 277)
½ medium	ripe banana
Finely crushed ice	

METHOD

Chill a large stemmed glass. Fill half a mixing jar with finely crushed ice. Add the other ingredients and blend but DO NOT STRAIN.

Variations: Frozen Strawberry Daiquiri: replace the banana with ½ cup of thawed frozen strawberries.

B52

INGREDIENTS **Serves 1**

15ml	Kahlua
15ml	amaretto
15ml	Bailey's Irish Cream

METHOD

Layer the Kahlua, amaretto and Bailey's Irish Cream in a shot glass in the given order.

Kiwi Margarita

INGREDIENTS

Serves 4

½ cup	kiwi pulp
½ cup	powdered sugar
3-4 tbsp	lemon juice
120 ml	tequila
30 ml	triple sec (optional)
30 ml	kiwi liqueur
¾ cup	crushed ice

To garnish
3-4 kiwi slices

METHOD

In a blender jar, combine all the ingredients and blend until frothy. Frost 4 Margarita glasses with powdered sugar. Pour into the prepared glasses and garnish with kiwi slices. Serve immediately.

Note: To give a foamy appearance to the drink, beat 1 egg white till stiff and fold into the drink before pouring into the glasses.

Fuzzy Navel

INGREDIENTS

Serves 1

120 ml	peach schnapps
120 ml	orange juice
120 ml	lemonade
Ice cubes	

METHOD

Pour all the ingredients into a Collins glass. Top with ice cubes and serve.

Pimm's No.1
Kiwi Margarita
Long Island Iced Tea

French Connection

INGREDIENTS **Serves 1**

45 ml brandy
15 ml amaretto
Ice cubes

METHOD

Fill an Old-fashioned glass with ice. Pour in the amaretto and the brandy. Stir and serve.

Long Island Iced Tea

INGREDIENTS **Serves 1**

10 ml vodka
10 ml gin
10 ml tequila
10 ml light rum
10 ml Cointreau
80 ml lemon juice
Coca Cola, as required

METHOD

Fill a Collins glass with crushed ice. Pour the spirits and lemon juice over the ice. Add Coca Cola until the drink becomes tea-coloured.

Greyhound

INGREDIENTS **Serves 1**

30 ml vodka
Grapefruit juice, as required
Ice cubes

METHOD

Fill a highball glass with ice cubes. Pour in the vodka, fill up with grapefruit juice and serve.

Irish Coffee

INGREDIENTS **Serves 2**

4	orange peel strips
4	lemon peel strips
16	whole cloves
1	4-inch cinnamon stick
2 tsp	sugar
60 ml	Irish whiskey
1½ cups	hot strong coffee
3 tbsp	whipped cream

Some powdered caster sugar

METHOD

Stud the orange and lemon peels with 2 cloves each and place in a frying pan or chafing dish with the cinnamon stick and the sugar. Cook over moderate heat, stirring occasionally with a wooden spoon, until the sugar melts. Pour the Irish whiskey into the pan and light a match to the liquid. (Be sure to step back since the flame will flare up instantly.) Shake the pan to and fro slowly until the flame dies out. Pour in the hot coffee all at once and bring to a simmer. Remove from heat.

Rub the cut edge of a strip of lemon peel around the inside of each Irish coffee cup and dip it into the caster sugar so that the sugar adheres to the inside rim. Pour in the coffee, trying not to disturb the sugar. Top with a dollop of whipped cream.

Mai Tai

INGREDIENTS **Serves 1**

1/6	lime
45 ml	very dark rum
45 ml	light rum
20 ml	orange liqueur (such as triple sec)
60 ml	pineapple juice

Juice of ¼ orange
¼ lemon
Sugar to taste (optional).
Ice cubes

To garnish
Orange slice

METHOD
Squeeze the lime into a highball glass filled with ice. Add the rest of the ingredients. Garnish with a slice of orange and serve.

Margarita

INGREDIENTS **Serves 4**

120 ml	tequila
60 ml	triple sec or Cointreau
½ cup	lemon juice
½ cup	powdered sugar
¾ cup	crushed ice
1	egg white, stiffly beaten (optional)

METHOD
Thoroughly chill 4 stemmed glasses. Frost the glass rims with coarse salt. In a blender, combine the tequila, triple sec, lemon juice, sugar and crushed ice. Whisk until frothy and well blended. Fold in the egg white to give a frothy appearance and pour into the prepared glasses.

Variations:
Strawberry Margarita: Add ½ cup fresh strawberry pulp and reduce lemon juice to ¼ cup. Decorate the glasses with sliced strawberries on the rim.

Kiwi Margarita: Add ½ cup kiwi pulp or ¼ cup kiwi liqueur and ¼ cup lemon juice.

Martini

INGREDIENTS **Serves 1**

¾ tsp	dry vermouth
60 ml	gin
Ice cubes	

To garnish
1 green olive

METHOD

Fill a mixing glass with ice. Add the vermouth and gin, stir gently and strain. Serve in a stemmed cocktail glass and garnish with an olive.

Millenium Punch

INGREDIENTS **Serves 1**

30 ml	Campari
30 ml	vodka
15 ml	Cointreau
60 ml	lemonade or bitter lemon
60 ml	orange juice
1 tsp	lemon juice
4-5	ice cubes
Soda water, as required	

To garnish
Slice of an orange

METHOD

Place ice cubes in a very tall glass and layer all the ingredients in the order given. Serve with a swizzle stick and orange slice.

Note: This makes an excellent poolside drink.

Papaya Daiquiri

INGREDIENTS **Serves 2**

1½ cups	chopped ripe papaya
1½ cups	crushed ice
2-3 tbsp	lemon juice
½ cup	sugar syrup
60 ml	white rum

To garnish
Lemon wedges and mint leaves

METHOD

Frost the rim of two stemmed glasses by dipping in water and then in powdered sugar. In a cocktail shaker or blender, mix all the ingredients and shake or blend until mixed well. Pour into the prepared glasses, garnish with lemon wedges and mint leaves.

Passion Beach

INGREDIENTS **Serves 1**

30 ml	Passoa
20 ml	peach schnapps
20 ml	Bacardi Limon
80 ml	grapefruit juice
20 ml	orange juice
Ice cubes	

To garnish
Fresh fruit slices

METHOD

Pour all the ingredients with ice cubes into a cocktail shaker. Shake well to mix. Strain into a highball glass. Garnish with fresh fruit fixed on the rim of the glass.

Peach Daiquiri

INGREDIENTS **Serves 1**

½ cup	chopped peaches
2 tbsp	lemon juice
2 tbsp	powdered sugar
30 ml	white rum

Crushed ice

To garnish

Mint sprigs and lemon slices

METHOD

Put all the ingredients into a blender and blend until frothy. Pour into a chilled stemmed glass, garnish with mint and lemon slices and serve.

Pimms No. 1

INGREDIENTS **Serves 1**

30 ml	Pimms
15 ml	vodka (optional)
150 ml	lemonade
60 ml	soda water
2-3 tbsp	chopped mixed fruit (apple, pear, kiwi, sweet lime, orange, banana etc.)

A dash of lemon juice
A few mint leaves
Ice cubes

METHOD

Pour the Pimms and vodka into a tall glass. Add lemonade and soda and mix well. Add a dash of lemon juice and top with chopped fruit, mint leaves and ice.

Jamaican Rum Punch

INGREDIENTS **Serves 8-10**

1 cup	151 proof rum (such as Bacardi)
½ cup	dark rum (such as Myers)
¼ cup	coconut rum (such as Malibu)
2½ cups	pineapple juice
2½ cups	orange juice
¼ cup	lime juice
3 tbsp	grenadine
Ice cubes	

METHOD

Mix all the ingredients together in a blender or punch bowl. Serve in stemmed glasses.

Note: This is a great summertime drink and a favourite of the rum lover.

Kamikaze

INGREDIENTS **Serves 1**

30 ml	vodka
15 ml	lime juice
15 ml	triple sec

METHOD

Pour all the ingredients into a shot or cordial glass and serve.

Vodka Tonic

INGREDIENTS **Serves 1**

45 ml vodka
Tonic water, as required

To garnish
A slice of lemon

METHOD

Pour the vodka into a highball glass. Top up with tonic water and garnish with a slice of lemon.

Whiskey Sour

INGREDIENTS **Serves 1**

45 ml blended whiskey
3 tbsp lemon juice
Crushed ice

To garnish
A cherry and a slice of orange

METHOD

Pour all the ingredients into a cocktail shaker. Shake well and pour into a stemmed glass. Serve with a cherry and a slice of orange.

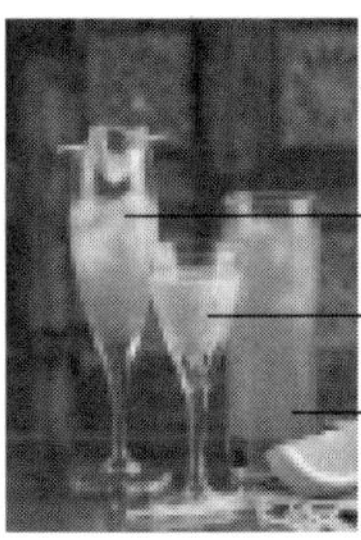

Whiskey Sour
Russian Roulade
Tequila Sunrise

Pina Colada

INGREDIENTS **Serves 4**

60 ml	light rum
1 cup	cream of coconut or thick coconut milk
2 cups	pineapple juice
Crushed ice	

To garnish

Pineapple slices and cherries threaded together on a cocktail stick

METHOD

Blend all the ingredients together with ice. Pour into stemmed glasses and garnish each glass with a cherry and pineapple slice on a toothpick. Serve with a straw.

Wine Cooler

INGREDIENTS **Serves 1**

¾ glass	red or white wine
¼ glass	ginger ale
A splash of any fruit juice	

METHOD

Pour all the ingredients into a mixing glass. Stir and pour into a wine glass or a highball glass.

Russian Roulade

INGREDIENTS **Serves 1**

15 ml	vodka
15 ml	Bailey's Irish Cream
15 ml	Grand Marnier

METHOD

Pour all the ingredients into a cordial or liqueur glass and serve.

Sangria

INGREDIENTS **Serves 6 glasses**

1 cup	water
½ cup	rock sugar
1 tsp	cinnamon Or
1	1-inch cinnamon stick
2	oranges, sliced
1	lemon, sliced
1	bottle medium-dry red wine
90 ml	brandy (optional)

To serve

1 cup finely chopped fruit (apple, strawberries, orange, kiwi etc.)

METHOD

Combine water, rock sugar and cinnamon in a saucepan. Cook over medium heat until the ingredients dissolve and form a syrup. Place the sliced fruit in a bowl and pour the syrup over. Leave to stand for 2 or more hours at room temperature. To serve, place ice cubes in a large jug. Add the syrup and fruit, wine and brandy, if using. Stir until the jug is frosted. Add chopped fresh fruit on top, and serve chilled.

Scorpion

INGREDIENTS

Makes 1 glass

60 ml	white run
15 ml	brandy
15 ml	lemon juice
60 ml	orange juice
1	sugar cube
2	ice cubes

METHOD

Blend all the ingredients . Serve in a stemmed glass.

Screw Driver

INGREDIENTS

Serves 1

30 ml vodka

Orange juice, as required

METHOD

Pour the vodka into a highball glass and top up with orange juice. Serve at once.

Shandy

INGREDIENTS **Makes 1 glass**

300 ml chilled beer
Splash of chilled 7 Up or lemonade

To garnish
1 lime wedge

METHOD

Pour chilled beer into a Plisner glass or a beer mug. Top it up with 7 Up or lemonade. Garnish with lime wedge and serve.

Silver Bullet

INGREDIENTS **Serves 1**

15 ml vodka
15 ml sambuca

METHOD

Pour the ingredients into a shot glass and serve.

Singapore Sling

INGREDIENTS

30 ml	gin
15 ml	grenadine
45 ml	Sweet and Sour Mix (page 277)
15 ml	cherry-flavoured brandy

Soda water, as required

To garnish

Cherry and a slice of orange

METHOD

Fill a Collins glass with ice. Pour in the gin, grenadine and sweet and sour mix. Stir lightly. Fill with soda and top with the cherry brandy. Garnish with the cherry and orange slice.

South of the Border

INGREDIENTS

Serves 1

30 ml	tequila
15 ml	brandy
15 ml	Tia Maria

A dash of white or rosé wine

METHOD

Pour all the ingredients into a cocktail shaker. Shake well and pour into an Old-fashioned or Rocks glass.

Strawberry Margarita

INGREDIENTS **Serves 4**

½ cup	strawberry pulp
½ cup	powdered sugar
3-4 tbsp	lemon juice
¾ cup	crushed ice

To garnish

3-4 whole strawberries

METHOD

In a blender jar, combine all the ingredients and blend until frothy. Frost 4 margarita glasses with powdered sugar. Pour the mixture into the prepared glasses and garnish with strawberries. Serve immediately.

Note: To give a foamy look to the drink, beat 1 egg white till stiff and fold into the drink before pouring into the glasses.

Variation: Replace strawberry pulp with peach pulp for a Peach Margarita.

Tequila Sunrise

INGREDIENTS **Serves 1**

30 ml	tequila
15 ml	grenadine

Orange juice, as required

Ice cubes

METHOD

Fill a highball glass with ice. Add the tequila and fill the glass up with orange juice. Top with the grenadine.

Tootsie Roll

INGREDIENTS **Serves 1**

30 ml	brown crème de cacao

Orange juice, as required
Ice cubes

METHOD

Fill a highball glass with ice. Pour in the crème de cacao and top up with orange juice. Stir well and serve.

Planter's Punch Bowl

INGREDIENTS **Serves 10-12**

3 cups	orange juice, chilled
3 cups	pineapple juice, chilled
1½ cups	lemon juice, chilled
1 cup	fresh lime juice, chilled
1 cup	light rum (such as Bacardi)
1 cup	peach schnapps
½ cup	powdered sugar

To serve and garnish
Ice Ring (recipe follows)
Cherries, mint leaves and lemon slices.

METHOD

Combine all the juices, rum and sugar in a punch bowl. Float the ice ring in the punch.

Ice Ring

Choose a ring mould to suit your punch bowl. Place it in the freezer until well chilled. Rinse the inside with cold water; return to the freezer until a thin coating of ice forms. Arrange the cherries and mint leaves, evenly spaced in the ring mould. Slowly, add enough water to cover the cherries. Freeze until firm. Remove from the freezer and arrange lemon slices directly over the cherries. Add enough water to cover. Freeze until firm. Fill the mould once again to the top with cold water and freeze until firm. When ready to use, run cold water on the outside of the mould to loosen it and then unmould. Float the ring in the punch bowl.

Glossary

Glossary of Selected Ingredients and Cooking Terms

Appetisers — A small dish of food or a drink before a meal

Bake — To cook in an oven by dry heat

Basil — Fresh or dried, broken or ground leaves with a pungent flavour and sweet aroma

Baste — To moisten with gravy or melted fat/butter during cooking

Bay leaf — Whole dried leaf or ground, with a strong flavour especially if the whole leaf is torn or crushed

Bean curd — Tofu or soybean cake

Beat — To introduce air into a mixture, e.g. egg yolks or cake batter, either with a spatula or electric beater

Blanch — To immerse briefly in boiling water

Broil — To cook directly over or above heat e.g. to grill

Canapé — An appetiser consisting of a firm base of bread, toast, pastry etc with a savoury and decorative topping

Chaat masala — A mixture of spice powders like salt, dried mango powder, chilli powder etc.

Chives — A member of the onion family. It has long spiky leaves

Croquette — A soft mixture of vegetables and seasoning, rolled into oval shapes coated with breadcrumbs or vermicelli and fried

Croutons — Small pieces of bread, fried or toasted

Crudités — A variety of fresh raw vegetables cut into fingers and served ice cold with a dip

Deep-fry — To fry in plenty of fat

Drain — To remove excess liquid or fat from food, usually with the help of a colander, or by placing on absorbent paper

Drizzle — To pour liquid slowly in a thin stream over food, e.g. vegetables with olive oil

Dropping consistency — When a mixture such as batter is too thick to pour, but will fall from a spoon in lumps.

Dry-roast — To heat or lightly fry; usually spices, on a griddle (tawa)

Dust — To sprinkle lightly with flour or sugar

Falafel — Dumplings made from assorted pluses or vegetables

Flambé — To ignite alcohol and pour the burning liquor on the finished dish

Fold in	To combine a light whisked mixture with other ingredients so that it retains its lightness
Fondue	A dish cooked on the table usually over a spirit heater. A Swiss fondue is a mixture of melted cheese and wine served with chunks of bread
Fritter	A portion of batter-coated food, deep-fried until crisp
Galangal	Thai ginger
Garam Masala	A mixture of ground spices
Garnish	To decorate food
Gelatine	Unflavoured jelly granules used to set the mixture
Glaze	To brush fat or liquid over food to give it a glossy look
Grenadine	Pomegranate syrup
Grease	To coat the surface of a dish with fat to prevent sticking
Grill	To cook over or under dry heat; barbecue
Jalapeño chillies	Spicy Mexican green chillies
Kaffir lime leaves	Leaves of the Thai lime tree, used for flavouring in Thai food
Malgapudi Chutney	A South Indian ground mixture of assorted lentils and spices
Marinate	To soak an ingredient before cooking in a mixture of spices or souring agents such as lemon juice or yogurt
Monterey Jack cheese	Tangy Mexican cheese
Mozzarella cheese	Special tangy Italian cheese used widely for pizzas
MSG	Monosodium Glutamate; a seasoning often used to flavour Chinese food
Munk pan	Heavy cast iron pan with depressions
Oregano	Dried or fresh leaves with a strong flavour
Parboil	To partially cook by boiling briefly in water
Pâté	A minced or finely chopped savoury purée sealed in a mould and served as a dip or spread
Pita bread	Lebanese flat bread either made with plain flour or wholewheat flour
Purée	To make a smooth pulp of vegetables or fruit usually in a blender
Quiche	An open custard tart with savoury or sweet filling
Raw sugar	Unrefined white sugar

Refresh	To run cold water over blanched food
Roulade	A soufflé-type mixture baked and served in a roll with various fillings
Sauté	To fry quickly in a little hot oil
Seasoning	Salt, pepper, spices, herbs etc. added to give depth of flavour
Sieve	To rub or press moist or dry food through a sieve
Simmer	To cook food gently in liquid just below boiling point.
Steam	To cook an ingredient in the steam of boiling water without it touching water
Stir-fry	To fry quickly over high heat in a lightly oiled pan (as in a wok), while stirring continuously
Sun-dried tomatoes	Tomatoes that are dried in the sun for a number of days and then stored or preserved in olive oil
Taco seasoning	A special blend of Mexican spice that is a combination of dried onion, garlic, chilies and other spices
Tahina	Sesame seed paste
Tarragon	Fresh or dried herb with a sweet, aromatic and piquant flavour
Thalipeeth flour	Mixed roasted grain flour
Thyme	Fresh or dried or ground herb with a pungent and aromatic flavour
Togorashi	Japanese 7-spice mix
Tortilla	Thin Mexican flat bread made with maize flour or plain flour
Toss	To mix ingredients in a quick, light way, till thoroughly blended
Tostada	Tortilla fried until crisp and served flat, topped with beans or a savoury mixture
Vinegar	Generally made from malt, cider, sugarcane or grape juice to add a sour taste to dishes
Whisk	To whip or beat ingredients to incorporate air and make light e.g. egg whites, yogurt or cream
Wok	A Chinese cooking pan like a kadai

Glossary of Indian Terms

Aniseed	Saunf
Asafoetida	Hing
Basil	Tulsi
Beaten rice	Poha
Bengal gram	Chana
Bengal gram, roasted	Bhuna chana
Bengal gram, split	Chane ki dal
Bengal gram flour	Besan
Black peppercorns	Kali mirch
Black salt	Kala namak
Black-eyed beans	Lobia/chauli
Black gram, whole	Sabut Udad
Black gram, skinless, split	Dhuli udad dal
Capsicum	Hari Shimla mirch
Caraway seeds	Shah jeera
Carom seeds	Ajwain
Chickpeas	Kabuli chana
Cinnamon	Dalchini
Clarified butter	Ghee
Coriander seeds	Dhania
Corn kernels	Makai ke dane
Cottage cheese	Paneer
Cumin seeds	Jeera
Curry leaves	Kadhi patte
Dark millet flour	Bajri atta
Dried fenugreek leaves	Kasoori methi
Dried mango powder	Aamchoor
Eggplant/aubergine	Baingan
Fenugreek leaves	Methi
Fenugreek seeds	Methi dana
Fresh millet	Ponk
Gram flour	Besan
Green gram, fresh	Hara chana
Green gram, split	Moong dal
Green gram, whole	Sabut moong
Green peas	Matar
Griddle	Tawa

Jaggery	Gud
Lentils, split	Masoor ki dal
Lotus seed puffs	Makhana
Millet	Bajra
Mustard	Rai or sarso
Nigella seeds (onion seeds)	Kalonji
Peanuts	Moongphali
Pine nuts	Chilgoza
Pink yam	Zimikand
Plain flour	Maida
Plum	Aloobukhara
Pomegranate	Anaar
Raisins	Kishmish
Red/yellow pepper	Lal/peeli Shimla mirch
Rock salt	Sendha namak
Rock sugar	Mishri
Sago	Sabudana
Semolina	Rawa or sooji
Sesame seeds	Til
Split Bengal gram	Chane ki dal
Spring onions (scallions)	Hara pyaaz
White millet flour	Jowar atta
Yogurt	Dahi

Conversion Table

1 teaspoon.............................5 ml

1 tablespoon.........................15 ml

1 peg/shot/1 fl oz..............30 ml

1 cup.....................................250 ml

1 litre.....................................1000 ml